Workshop on Semi-Supervised Learning for Natural Language Processing 2009

Held at NAACL HLT 2009

Boulder, Colorado, USA
4 June 2009

ISBN: 978-1-61738-564-3

Printed from e-media with permission by:

Curran Associates, Inc.
57 Morehouse Lane
Red Hook, NY 12571
www.proceedings.com

Some format issues inherent in the e-media version may also appear in this print version.

Printed by Curran Associates, Inc. (2010)

Association for Computational Linguistics
209 N. Eighth Street
Stroudsburg, Pennsylvania 18360

Phone: 1-570-476-8006
Fax: 1-570-476-0860

acl@aclweb.org

Introduction

Welcome to the NAACL HLT Workshop on Semi-supervised Learning for Natural Language Processing!

Will semi-supervised learning (SSL) become the next de-facto standard for building natural language processing (NLP) systems, just as supervised learning has transformed the field in the last decade? Or will it remain as a nice idea that doesn't always work in practice? Semi-supervised learning has become an important topic due to the promise that high-quality labeled data and abundant unlabeled data, if leveraged appropriately, can achieve superior performance at lower cost. As researchers in semi-supervised learning reach critical mass, we believe it is time to take a step back and think broadly about whether we can discover general insights from the various techniques developed for different NLP tasks.

The goal of this workshop is to help build a community of SSL-NLP researchers and foster discussions about insights, speculations, and results (both positive and negative) that may otherwise not appear in a technical paper at a major conference. In our call-for-paper, we posed some open questions:

1. Problem Structure: What are the different classes of NLP problem structures (e.g. sequences, trees, N-best lists) and what algorithms are best suited for each class? For instance, can graph-based algorithms be successfully applied to sequence-to-sequence problems like machine translation, or are self-training and feature-based methods the only reasonable choices for these problems?

2. Background Knowledge: What kinds of NLP-specific background knowledge can we exploit to aid semi-supervised learning? Recent learning paradigms such as constraint-driven learning and prototype learning take advantage of our domain knowledge about particular NLP tasks; they represent a move away from purely data-agnostic methods and are good examples of how linguistic intuition can drive algorithm development.

3. Scalability: NLP data-sets are often large. What are the scalability challenges and solutions for applying existing semi-supervised learning algorithms to NLP data?

4. Evaluation and Negative Results: What can we learn from negative results? Can we make an educated guess as to when semi-supervised learning might outperform supervised or unsupervised learning based on what we know about the NLP problem?

5. To Use or Not To Use: Should semi-supervised learning only be employed in low-resource languages/tasks (i.e. little labeled data, much unlabeled data), or should we expect gains even in high-resource scenarios (i.e. expecting semi-supervised learning to improve on a supervised system that is already more than 95% accurate)?

We received 17 submissions and selected 10 papers after a rigorous review process. These papers cover a variety of tasks, ranging from information extraction to speech recognition. Some introduce new techniques, while others compared existing methods under a variety of situations. We are pleased to present these papers in this volume.

Our workshop will be kicked off with a keynote talk by Jason Eisner (Johns Hopkins University). We will end with a panel discussion on the future of SSL-NLP, which will feature invited position papers from several prominent researchers. (Some are included in this volume; others will be online at the workshop website: http://sites.google.com/site/sslnlp/).

We are especially grateful to the program committee for their hard work and the presenters for their excellent papers. We would also like to thank the following people for their many help and support: Hal Daume, Sajib Dasgupta, Jason Eisner, Nizar Habash, Mark Hasegawa-Johnson, Andrew McCallum, Vincent Ng, Anoop Sarkar, Eric Ringger, and Jerry Zhu.

Best regards,

Qin Iris Wang, Kevin Duh, Dekang Lin
SSL-NLP Workshop Organizers

26 April 2009

Organizers:

Qin Iris Wang, AT&T
Kevin Duh, University of Washington
Dekang Lin, Google Research

Program Committee:

Steven Abney (University of Michigan, USA)
Yasemin Altun (Max Planck Institute for Biological Cybernetics, Germany)
Tim Baldwin (University of Melbourne, Australia)
Shane Bergsma (University of Alberta, Canada)
Antal van den Bosch (Tilburg University, The Netherlands)
John Blitzer (UC Berkeley, USA)
Ming-Wei Chang (UIUC, USA)
Walter Daelemans (University of Antwerp, Belgium)
Hal Daume III (University of Utah, USA)
Kevin Gimpel (Carnegie Mellon University, USA)
Andrew Goldberg (University of Wisconsin, USA)
Liang Huang (Google Research, USA)
Rie Johnson [formerly, Ando] (RJ Research Consulting)
Katrin Kirchhoff (University of Washington, USA)
Percy Liang (UC Berkeley, USA)
Gary Geunbae Lee (POSTECH, Korea)
Gina-Anne Levow (University of Chicago, USA)
Gideon Mann (Google, USA)
David McClotsky (Brown University, USA)
Ray Mooney (UT Austin, USA)
Hwee Tou Ng (National University of Singapore, Singapore)
Vincent Ng (UT Dallas, USA)
Miles Osborne (University of Edinburgh, UK)
Mari Ostendorf (University of Washington, USA)
Chris Pinchak (University of Alberta, Canada)
Dragomir Radev (University of Michigan, USA)
Dan Roth (UIUC, USA)
Anoop Sarkar (Simon Fraser University, Canada)
Dale Schuurmans (University of Alberta, Canada)
Akira Shimazu (JAIST, Japan)
Jun Suzuki (NTT, Japan)
Yee Whye Teh (University College London, UK)
Kristina Toutanova (Microsoft Research, USA)
Jason Weston (NEC, USA)
Tong Zhang (Rutgers University, USA)

Ming Zhou (Microsoft Research Asia, China)
Xiaojin (Jerry) Zhu (University of Wisconsin, USA)

Invited Speaker:

Jason Eisner, Johns Hopkins University

Table of Contents

Conference Program

Thursday, June 4, 2009

8:30–9:00 Coffee Service

9:00–9:10 Opening Remarks

9:10–10:10 Invited Talk by Jason Eisner

10:10–10:30 *Coupling Semi-Supervised Learning of Categories and Relations*
Andrew Carlson, Justin Betteridge, Estevam Rafael Hruschka Junior and Tom M. Mitchell

10:30–11:00 Morning Break

11:00–11:20 *Surrogate Learning - From Feature Independence to Semi-Supervised Classification*
Sriharsha Veeramachaneni and Ravi Kumar Kondadadi

11:25–11:45 *Keepin' It Real: Semi-Supervised Learning with Realistic Tuning*
Andrew B. Goldberg and Xiaojin Zhu

11:50–12:10 *Is Unlabeled Data Suitable for Multiclass SVM-based Web Page Classification?*
Arkaitz Zubiaga, Víctor Fresno and Raquel Martínez

12:15–12:35 *A Comparison of Structural Correspondence Learning and Self-training for Discriminative Parse Selection*
Barbara Plank

12:35–2:00 Lunch Break

2:00–2:20 *Latent Dirichlet Allocation with Topic-in-Set Knowledge*
David Andrzejewski and Xiaojin Zhu

2:25–2:45 *An Analysis of Bootstrapping for the Recognition of Temporal Expressions*
Jordi Poveda, Mihai Surdeanu and Jordi Turmo

2:50–3:10 *A Simple Semi-supervised Algorithm For Named Entity Recognition*
Wenhui Liao and Sriharsha Veeramachaneni

Thursday, June 4, 2009 (continued)

3:15–3:35 *Can One Language Bootstrap the Other: A Case Study on Event Extraction*
Zheng Chen and Heng Ji

3:35–4:00 Afternoon Break

4:00–4:20 *On Semi-Supervised Learning of Gaussian Mixture Models for Phonetic Classification*
Jui-Ting Huang and Mark Hasegawa-Johnson

4:25–5:25 Panel Discusstion

Discriminative Models for Semi-Supervised Natural Language Learning
Sajib Dasgupta and Vincent Ng

5:25–5:40 Workshop Wrap-up

Coupling Semi-Supervised Learning of Categories and Relations

Andrew Carlson[1], Justin Betteridge[1], Estevam R. Hruschka Jr.[1,2] and Tom M. Mitchell[1]
[1]School of Computer Science
Carnegie Mellon University
Pittsburgh, PA 15213
{acarlson,jbetter,tom.mitchell}@cs.cmu.edu
[2]Federal University of Sao Carlos
Sao Carlos, SP - Brazil
estevam@dc.ufscar.br

Abstract

We consider semi-supervised learning of information extraction methods, especially for extracting instances of noun categories (e.g., 'athlete,' 'team') and relations (e.g., 'playsForTeam(athlete,team)'). Semi-supervised approaches using a small number of labeled examples together with many unlabeled examples are often unreliable as they frequently produce an internally consistent, but nevertheless incorrect set of extractions. We propose that this problem can be overcome by simultaneously learning classifiers for many different categories and relations in the presence of an ontology defining constraints that couple the training of these classifiers. Experimental results show that simultaneously learning a coupled collection of classifiers for 30 categories and relations results in much more accurate extractions than training classifiers individually.

1 Introduction

A great wealth of knowledge is expressed on the web in natural language. Translating this into a structured knowledge base containing facts about entities (e.g., 'Disney') and relations between those entities (e.g. CompanyIndustry('Disney', 'entertainment')) would be of great use to many applications. Although fully supervised methods for learning to extract such facts from text work well, the cost of collecting many labeled examples of each type of knowledge to be extracted is impractical. Researchers have also explored semi-supervised learning methods that rely primarily on unlabeled data, but these approaches tend to suffer from the fact that they face an under-constrained learning task, resulting in extractions that are often inaccurate.

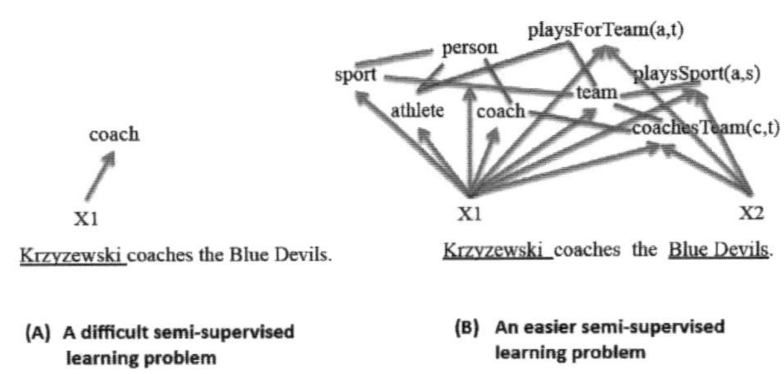

Figure 1: We show that significant improvements in accuracy result from coupling the training of information extractors for many inter-related categories and relations (B), compared with the simpler but much more difficult task of learning a single information extractor (A).

We present an approach to semi-supervised learning that yields more accurate results by coupling the training of many information extractors. The intuition behind our approach (summarized in Figure 1) is that semi-supervised training of a single type of extractor such as 'coach' is much more difficult than simultaneously training many extractors that cover a variety of inter-related entity and relation types. In particular, prior knowledge about the relationships between these different entities and relations (e.g., that 'coach(x)' implies 'person(x)' and 'not sport(x)') allows unlabeled data to become a much more useful constraint during training.

Although previous work has coupled the learning of multiple categories, or used static category recognizers to check arguments for learned relation ex-

Proceedings of the NAACL HLT Workshop on Semi-supervised Learning for Natural Language Processing, pages 1–9,
Boulder, Colorado, June 2009.

tractors, our work is the first we know of to couple the simultaneous semi-supervised training of multiple categories and relations. Our experiments show that this coupling results in more accurate extractions. Based on our results reported here, we hypothesize that significant accuracy improvements in information extraction will be possible by coupling the training of hundreds or thousands of extractors.

2 Problem Statement

It will be helpful to first explain our use of common terms. An *ontology* is a collection of unary and binary predicates, also called *categories* and *relations*, respectively.[1] An *instance* of a category, or a *category instance*, is a noun phrase; an instance of a relation, or a *relation instance*, is a pair of noun phrases. Instances can be *positive* or *negative* with respect to a specific predicate, meaning that the predicate holds or does not hold for that particular instance. A *promoted instance* is an instance which our algorithm believes to be a positive instance of some predicate. Also associated with both categories and relations are *patterns*: strings of tokens with placeholders (e.g., 'game against *arg1*' and '*arg1* , head coach of *arg2*'). A *promoted pattern* is a pattern believed to be a high-probability indicator for some predicate.

The challenge addressed by this work is to learn extractors to automatically populate the categories and relations of a specified ontology with high-confidence instances, starting from a few seed positive instances and patterns for each predicate and a large corpus of sentences annotated with part-of-speech (POS) tags. We focus on extracting facts that are stated multiple times in the corpus, which we can assess probabilistically using corpus statistics. We do not resolve strings to real-world entities— the problems of synonym resolution and disambiguation of strings that can refer to multiple entities are left for future work.

3 Related Work

Work on multitask learning has demonstrated that supervised learning of multiple "related" functions together can yield higher accuracy than learning the functions separately (Thrun, 1996; Caruana, 1997). Semi-supervised multitask learning has been shown to increase accuracy when tasks are related, allowing one to use a prior that encourages similar parameters (Liu et al., 2008). Our work also involves semi-supervised training of multiple coupled functions, but differs in that we assume explicit prior knowledge of the precise way in which our multiple functions are related (e.g., that the values of the functions applied to the same input are mutually exclusive, or that one implies the other).

In this paper, we focus on a 'bootstrapping' method for semi-supervised learning. Bootstrapping approaches start with a small number of labeled 'seed' examples, use those seed examples to train an initial model, then use this model to label some of the unlabeled data. The model is then retrained, using the original seed examples plus the self-labeled examples. This process iterates, gradually expanding the amount of labeled data. Such approaches have shown promise in applications such as web page classification (Blum and Mitchell, 1998), named entity classification (Collins and Singer, 1999), parsing (McClosky et al., 2006), and machine translation (Ueffing, 2006).

Bootstrapping approaches to information extraction can yield impressive results with little initial human effort (Brin, 1998; Agichtein and Gravano, 2000; Ravichandran and Hovy, 2002; Pasca et al., 2006). However, after many iterations, they usually suffer from semantic drift, where errors in labeling accumulate and the learned concept 'drifts' from what was intended (Curran et al., 2007). Coupling the learning of predicates by using positive examples of one predicate as negative examples for others has been shown to help limit this drift (Riloff and Jones, 1999; Yangarber, 2003). Additionally, ensuring that relation arguments are of certain, expected types can help mitigate the promotion of incorrect instances (Paşca et al., 2006; Rosenfeld and Feldman, 2007). Our work builds on these ideas to couple the simultaneous bootstrapped training of multiple categories and multiple relations.

Our approach to information extraction is based on using high precision contextual patterns (e.g., 'is mayor of *arg1*' suggests that *arg1* is a city). An early pattern-based approach to information extraction acquired 'is a' relations from text using generic contextual patterns (Hearst, 1992). This approach was later scaled up to the web by Etzioni et al. (2005).

[1] We do not consider predicates of higher arity in this work.

Other research explores the task of 'open information extraction', where the predicates to be learned are not specified in advance (Shinyama and Sekine, 2006; Banko et al., 2007), but emerge instead from analysis of the data. In contrast, our approach relies strongly on knowledge in the ontology about the predicates to be learned, and relationships among them, in order to achieve high accuracy.

Chang et al. (2007) present a framework for learning that optimizes the data likelihood plus constraint-based penalty terms than capture prior knowledge, and demonstrate it with semi-supervised learning of segmentation models. Constraints that capture domain knowledge guide bootstrap learning of a structured model by penalizing or disallowing violations of those constraints. While similar in spirit, our work differs in that we consider learning many models, rather than one structured model, and that we are consider a much larger scale application in a different domain.

4 Approach

4.1 Coupling of Predicates

As mentioned above, our approach hinges on the notion of coupling the learning of multiple functions in order to constrain the semi-supervised learning problem we face. Our system learns four different types of functions. For each category c:

1. $f_{c,inst} : NP(\mathcal{C}) \rightarrow [0, 1]$
2. $f_{c,patt} : Patt_C(\mathcal{C}) \rightarrow [0, 1]$

and for each relation r:

1. $f_{r,inst} : NP(\mathcal{C}) \times NP(\mathcal{C}) \rightarrow [0, 1]$
2. $f_{r,patt} : Patt_R(\mathcal{C}) \rightarrow [0, 1]$

where $\mathcal{C}$ is the input corpus, $NP(\mathcal{C})$ is the set of valid noun phrases in $\mathcal{C}$, $Patt_C(\mathcal{C})$ is the set of valid category patterns in $\mathcal{C}$, and $Patt_R(\mathcal{C})$ is the set of valid relation patterns in $\mathcal{C}$. "Valid" noun phrases, category patterns, and relation patterns are defined in Section 4.2.2.

The learning of these functions is coupled in two ways:

1. Sharing among same-arity predicates according to logical relations
2. Relation argument type-checking

These methods of coupling are made possible by prior knowledge in the input ontology, beyond the lists of categories and relations mentioned above. We provide general descriptions of these methods of coupling in the next sections, while the details are given in section 4.2.

4.1.1 Sharing among same-arity predicates

Each predicate P in the ontology has a list of other same-arity predicates with which P is *mutually exclusive*, where $mutuallyExclusive(P, P') \equiv (P(arg1) \Rightarrow \neg P'(arg1)) \wedge (P'(arg1) \Rightarrow \neg P(arg1))$, and similarly for relations. These mutually exclusive relationships are used to carry out the following simple but crucial coupling: if predicate A is mutually exclusive with predicate B, A's positive instances *and* patterns become *negative instances* and *negative patterns* for B. For example, if 'city', having an instance 'Boston' and a pattern 'mayor of *arg1*', is mutually exclusive with 'scientist', then 'Boston' and 'mayor of *arg1*' will become a negative instance and a negative pattern respectively for 'scientist.' Such negative instances and patterns provide negative evidence to constrain the bootstrapping process and forestall divergence.

Some categories are declared to be a subset of one of the other categories being populated, where $subset(P, P') \equiv P(arg1) \Rightarrow P'(arg1)$, (e.g., 'athlete' is a subset of 'person'). This prior knowledge is used to share instances and patterns of the subcategory (e.g., 'athlete') as *positive* instances and patterns for the super-category (e.g., 'person').

4.1.2 Relation argument type-checking

The last type of prior knowledge we use to couple the learning of functions is *type checking* information which couples the learning of relations with categories. For example, the arguments of the 'ceoOf' relation are declared to be of the categories 'person' and 'company'. Our approach does not promote a pair of noun phrases as an instance of a relation unless the two noun phrases are classified as belonging to the correct argument types. Additionally, when a relation instance is promoted, the arguments become promoted instances of their respective categories.

4.2 Algorithm Description

In this section, we describe our algorithm, CBL (Coupled Bootstrap Learner), in detail.

The inputs to CBL are a large corpus of POS-tagged sentences and an initial ontology with pre-

Algorithm 1: CBL Algorithm

Input: An ontology $\mathcal{O}$, and text corpus C
Output: Trusted instances/patterns for each predicate

```
SHARE initial instances/patterns among
predicates;
for i = 1, 2, ..., ∞ do
  foreach predicate p ∈ O do
    EXTRACT candidate instances/patterns;
    FILTER candidates;
    TRAIN instance/pattern classifiers;
    ASSESS candidates using classifiers;
    PROMOTE highest-confidence candidates;
  end
  SHARE promoted items among predicates;
end
```

defined categories, relations, mutually exclusive relationships between same-arity predicates, subset relationships between some categories, seed instances for all predicates, and seed patterns for the categories. Categories in the input ontology also have a flag indicating whether instances must be proper nouns, common nouns, or whether they can be either (e.g., instances of 'city' are proper nouns).

Algorithm 1 gives a summary of the CBL algorithm. First, seed instances and patterns are shared among predicates using the available mutual exclusion, subset, and type-checking relations. Then, for an indefinite number of iterations, CBL expands the sets of promoted instances and patterns for each predicate, as detailed below.

CBL was designed to allow learning many predicates simultaneously from a large sample of text from the web. In each iteration of the algorithm, the information needed from the text corpus is gathered in two passes through the corpus using the MapReduce framework (Dean and Ghemawat, 2008). This allows us to complete an iteration of the system in 1 hour using a corpus containing millions of web pages (see Section 5.3 for details on the corpus).

4.2.1 Sharing

At the start of execution, seed instances and patterns are shared among predicates according to the mutual exclusion, subset, and type-checking constraints. Newly promoted instances and patterns are shared at the end of each iteration.

4.2.2 Candidate Extraction

CBL finds new candidate instances by using newly promoted patterns to extract the noun phrases that co-occur with those patterns in the text corpus. To keep the size of this set manageable, CBL limits the number of new candidate instances for each predicate to 1000 by selecting the ones that occur with the most newly promoted patterns. An analogous procedure is used to extract candidate patterns. Candidate extraction is performed for all predicates in a single pass through the corpus using the MapReduce framework.

The candidate extraction procedure has definitions for valid instances and patterns that limit extraction to instances that look like noun phrases and patterns that are likely to be informative. Here we provide brief descriptions of those definitions.

Category Instances In the placeholder of a category pattern, CBL looks for a noun phrase. It uses part-of-speech tags to segment noun phrases, ignoring determiners. Proper nouns containing prepositions are segmented using a reimplementation of the Lex algorithm (Downey et al., 2007). Category instances are only extracted if they obey the proper/common noun specification of the category.

Category Patterns If a promoted category instance is found in a sentence, CBL extracts the preceding words as a candidate pattern if they are verbs followed by a sequence of adjectives, prepositions, or determiners (e.g., 'being acquired by *arg1*') or nouns and adjectives followed by a sequence of adjectives, prepositions, or determiners (e.g., 'former CEO of *arg1*').

CBL extracts the words following the instance as a candidate pattern if they are verbs followed optionally by a noun phrase (e.g., '*arg1* broke the home run record'), or verbs followed by a preposition (e.g., '*arg1* said that').

Relation Instances If a promoted relation pattern (e.g., '*arg1* is mayor of *arg2*') is found, a candidate relation instance is extracted if both placeholders are valid noun phrases, and if they obey the proper/common specifications for their categories.

Relation Patterns If both arguments from a promoted relation instance are found in a sentence then the intervening sequence of words is extracted as a candidate relation pattern if it contains no more than 5 tokens, has a content word, has an uncapitalized word, and has at least one non-noun.

4.2.3 Candidate Filtering

Candidate instances and patterns are filtered to maintain high precision, and to avoid extremely specific patterns. An instance is only considered for assessment if it co-occurs with at least two promoted patterns in the text corpus, and if its co-occurrence count with all promoted patterns is at least three times greater than its co-occurrence count with negative patterns. Candidate patterns are filtered in the same manner using instances.

All co-occurrence counts needed by the filtering step are obtained with an additional pass through the corpus using MapReduce. This implementation is much more efficient than one that relies on web search queries. CBL typically requires co-occurrence counts of at least 10,000 instances with any of at least 10,000 patterns, which would require 100 million hit count queries.

4.2.4 Candidate Assessment

Next, for each predicate CBL trains a discretized Naïve Bayes classifier to classify the candidate instances. Its features include pointwise mutual information (PMI) scores (Turney, 2001) of the candidate instance with each of the positive and negative patterns associated with the class. The current sets of promoted and negative instances are used as training examples for the classifier. Attributes are discretized based on information gain (Fayyad and Irani, 1993).

Patterns are assessed using an estimate of the precision of each pattern p:

$$Precision(p) = \frac{\sum_{i \in \mathcal{I}} count(i,p)}{count(p)}$$

where $\mathcal{I}$ is the set of promoted instances for the predicate currently being considered, $count(i,p)$ is the co-occurrence count of instance i with pattern p, and $count(p)$ is the hit count of the pattern p. This is a pessimistic estimate because it assumes that the rest of the occurrences of pattern p are not with positive examples of the predicate. We also penalize extremely rare patterns by thresholding the denominator using the 25th percentile candidate pattern hit count (McDowell and Cafarella, 2006).

All of the co-occurrence counts needed for the assessment step are collected in the same MapReduce pass as those required for filtering candidates.

4.2.5 Candidate Promotion

CBL then ranks the candidates according to their assessment scores and promotes at most 100 instances and 5 patterns for each predicate.

5 Experimental Evaluation

We designed our experimental evaluation to try to answer the following questions: Can CBL iterate many times and still achieve high precision? How helpful are the types of coupling that we employ? Can we extend existing semantic resources?

5.1 Configurations of the Algorithm

We ran our algorithm in three configurations:

- Full: The algorithm as described in Section 4.2.
- No Sharing Among Same-Arity Predicates (NS): This configuration couples predicates only using type-checking constraints. It uses the full algorithm, except that predicates of the same arity do not share promoted instances and patterns with each other. Seed instances and patterns *are* shared, though, so each predicate has a small, fixed pool of negative evidence.
- No Category/Relation coupling (NCR): This configuration couples predicates using mutual exclusion and subset constraints, but not type-checking. It uses the full algorithm, except that relation instance arguments are not filtered or assessed using their specified categories, and arguments of promoted relations are not shared as promoted instances of categories. The only type-checking information used is the common/proper noun specifications of arguments for filtering out implausible instances.

5.2 Initial ontology

Our ontology contained categories and relations related to two domains: companies and sports. Extra categories were added to provide negative evidence to the domain-related categories: 'hobby' for 'economic sector'; 'actor,' 'politician,' and 'scientist' for 'athlete' and 'coach'; and 'board game' for 'sport'. Table 1 lists each predicate in the leftmost column. Categories were started with 10–20 seed

Predicate	5 iterations			10 iterations			15 iterations		
	Full	NS	NCR	Full	NS	NCR	Full	NS	NCR
Actor	93	100	100	93	97	100	100	97	100
Athlete	100	100	100	100	93	100	100	73	100
Board Game	93	76	93	89	27	93	89	30	93
City	100	100	100	100	97	100	100	100	100
Coach	100	63	73	97	53	43	97	47	47
Company	100	100	100	97	90	97	100	90	100
Country	60	40	60	30	43	27	40	23	40
Economic Sector	77	63	73	57	67	67	50	63	40
Hobby	67	63	67	40	40	57	20	23	30
Person	97	97	90	97	93	97	93	97	93
Politician	93	93	97	73	53	90	90	53	87
Product	97	87	90	90	87	100	97	90	77
Product Type	93	93	90	70	73	97	77	80	67
Scientist	100	90	97	97	63	97	93	60	100
Sport	100	90	100	93	67	83	97	27	90
Sports Team	100	97	100	97	70	100	90	50	100
Category Average	92	84	89	82	70	84	83	63	79
Acquired(Company, Company)	77	77	80	67	80	47	70	63	47
CeoOf(Person, Company)	97	87	100	90	87	97	90	80	83
CoachesTeam(Coach, Sports Team)	100	100	100	100	100	97	100	100	90
CompetesIn(Company, Econ. Sector)	97	97	80	100	93	67	97	63	60
CompetesWith(Company, Company)	93	80	60	77	70	37	70	60	43
HasOfficesIn(Company, City)	97	93	40	93	90	27	93	57	30
HasOperationsIn(Company, Country)	100	95	50	100	97	40	90	83	13
HeadquarteredIn(Company, City)	77	90	20	70	77	27	70	60	7
LocatedIn(City, Country)	90	67	57	63	50	43	73	50	30
PlaysFor(Athlete, Sports Team)	100	100	0	100	97	7	100	43	0
PlaysSport(Athlete, Sport)	100	100	27	93	80	10	100	40	30
TeamPlaysSport(Sports Team, Sport)	100	100	77	100	97	80	93	83	67
Produces(Company, Product)	91	83	90	83	93	67	93	80	57
HasType(Product, Product Type)	73	63	17	33	67	33	40	57	27
Relation Average	92	88	57	84	84	48	84	66	42
All	92	86	74	83	76	68	84	64	62

Table 1: Precision (%) for each predicate. Results are presented after 5, 10, and 15 iterations, for the Full, No Sharing (NS), and No Category/Relation Coupling (NCR) configurations of CBL . Note that we expect Full and NCR to perform similarly for categories, but for Full to outperform NCR on relations and for Full to outperform NS on both categories and relations.

instances and 5 seed patterns. The seed instances were specified by a human, and the seed patterns were derived from the generic patterns of Hearst for each predicate (Hearst, 1992). Relations were started with similar numbers of seed instances, and no seed patterns (it is less obvious how to generate good seed patterns from relation names). Most predicates were declared as mutually exclusive with most others, except for special cases (e.g., 'hobby' and 'sport'; 'university' and 'sports team'; and 'has offices in' and 'headquartered in').

5.3 Corpus

Our text corpus was from a 200-million page web crawl. We parsed the HTML, filtered out non-English pages using a stop word ratio threshold, then filtered out web spam and adult content using a 'bad word' list. The pages were then segmented into sentences, tokenized, and tagged with parts-of-speech using the OpenNLP package. Finally, we filtered the sentences to eliminate those that were likely to be noisy and not useful for learning (e.g., sentences without a verb, without any lowercase words, with too many words that were all capital letters). This yielded a corpus of roughly 514-million sentences.

5.4 Experimental Procedure

We ran each configuration for 15 iterations. To evaluate the precision of promoted instances, we sampled 30 instances from the promoted set for each predicate in each configuration after 5, 10, and 15 iterations, pooled together the samples for each predicate, and then judged their correctness. The judge did not know which run an instance was sampled from. We estimated the precision of the promoted instances from each run after 5, 10, and 15 iterations as the number of correct promoted instances divided by the number sampled. While samples of 30 instances do not produce tight confidence intervals around individual estimates, they are sufficient for testing for the effects in which we are interested.

5.5 Results

Table 1 shows the precision of each of the three algorithm configurations for each category and relation after 5, 10, and 15 iterations. As is apparent in this table, fully coupled training (Full) outperforms training when coupling is removed between categories and relations (NCR), and also when coupling is removed among predicates of the same arity (NS). The net effect is substantial, as is apparent from the bottom row of Table 1, which shows that the precision of Full outperforms NS by 6% and NCR by 18% after the first 5 iterations, and by an even larger 20% and 22% after 15 iterations. This increasing gap in precision as iterations increase reflects the ability of coupled learning to constrain the system to reduce the otherwise common drift associated with self-trained classifiers.

Using Student's paired t-test, we found that for categories, the difference in performance between Full and NS is statistically significant after 5, 10, and 15 iterations ($p\text{-value} < 0.05$).[2] No significant difference was found between Full and NCR for categories, but this is not a surprise, because NCR still uses mutually exclusive and subset constraints. The same test finds that the differences between Full and NS are significant for relations after 15 iterations, and the differences between Full and NCR are significant after 5, 10, and 15 iterations for relations.

The worst-performing categories after 15 iterations of Full are 'country,' 'economic sector,' and 'hobby.' The Full configuration of CBL promoted 1637 instances for 'country,' far more than the number of correct answers. Many of these are general geographic regions like 'Bayfield Peninsula' and 'Baltic Republics.' In the 'hobby' case, promoting patterns like 'the types of *arg1*' led to the category drifting into a general list of plural common nouns. 'Economic sector' drifted into academic fields like 'Behavioral Science' and 'Political Sciences.' We expect that the learning of these categories would be significantly better if there were even more categories being learned to provide additional negative evidence during the filtering and assessment steps of the algorithm.

At this stage of development, obtaining high recall is not a priority because our intent is to create a continuously running and continuously improving system; it is our hope that high recall will come with time. However, to very roughly convey the completeness of the current results we show in Table 2 the average number of instances promoted for cate-

[2]Our selection of the paired t-test was motivated by the work of Smucker et al. (2007), but the Wilcoxon signed rank test gives the same results.

Configuration	Categories Instances	Categories Prec.	Relations Instances	Relations Prec.
Full	970	83	191	84
NS	1337	63	307	66
NCR	916	79	458	42

Table 2: Average numbers of promoted category and relation instances and estimates of their precision for each configuration of CBL after 15 iterations.

Skype
isA: company
company_economic_sector: VoIP
competes_with: AOL, MSN, Yahoo, Google
acquired_by: Ebay

EBay
isA: company
company_CEO: Pierre Omidyar
competes_with: Dell, Google, Yahoo, Amazon, Amazon.com, Microsoft, AOL
acquired: PayPal, Skype

Figure 2: Extracted facts for two companies discovered by CBL Full. These two companies were extracted by the learned 'company' extractor, and the relations shown were extracted by learned relation extractors.

gories and relations for each of the three configurations of CBL after 15 iterations. For categories, not sharing examples results in fewer negative examples during the filtering and assessment steps. This yields more promoted instances on average. For relations, not using type checking yields higher relative recall, but at a much lower level of precision.

Figure 2 gives one view of the type of information extracted by the collection of learned category and relation classifiers. Note the initial seed examples provided to CBL did not include information about either company or any of these relation instances.[3]

5.6 Comparison to an Existing Database

To estimate the capacity of our algorithm to contribute additional facts to publicly available semantic resources, we compared the complete lists of instances promoted during the Full 15 iteration run for certain categories to corresponding lists in the Freebase database (Metaweb Technologies, 2009). Excluding the categories that did not have a directly corresponding Freebase list, we computed for each category: $Precision \times |CBLInstances| - |Matches|$, where $Precision$ is the estimated precision from our random sample of 30 instances, $|CBLInstances|$ is the total number of instances promoted for that category, and $|Matches|$ is the number of promoted instances that had an exact match in Freebase. While exact matches may underestimate the number of matches, it should be noted that rather than make definitive claims, our intent here is simply to give rough estimates, which are shown in Table 3. These approximate numbers indicate a potential to use CBL to extend existing semantic resources like Freebase.

[3]See `http://rtw.ml.cmu.edu/sslnlp09` for results from a full run of the system.

Category	Est. Prec.	CBL Instances	Freebase Matches	Est. New Instances
Actor	100	522	465	57
Athlete	100	117	54	63
Board Game	89	18	6	10
City	100	1799	1665	134
Company	100	1937	995	942
Econ. Sector	50	1541	137	634
Politician	90	962	74	792
Product	97	1259	0	1221
Sports Team	90	414	139	234
Sport	97	613	134	461

Table 3: Estimated numbers of "new instances" (correct instances promoted by CBL in the Full 15 iteration run which do not have a match in Freebase) and the values used in calculating them.

6 Conclusion

We have presented a method of coupling the semi-supervised learning of categories and relations and demonstrated empirically that the coupling forestalls the problem of semantic drift associated with bootstrap learning methods. We suspect that learning additional predicates simultaneously will yield even more accurate learning. An approximate comparison with an existing repository of semantic knowledge, Freebase, suggests that our methods can contribute new facts to existing resources.

Acknowledgments

This work is supported in part by DARPA, Google, a Yahoo! Fellowship to Andrew Carlson, and the Brazilian research agency CNPq. We also gratefully acknowledge Jamie Callan for making available his collection of web pages, Yahoo! for use of their M45 computing cluster, and the anonymous reviewers for their comments.

References

Eugene Agichtein and Luis Gravano. 2000. Snowball: Extracting relations from large plain-text collections. In *JCDL*.

Michele Banko, Michael J. Cafarella, Stephen Soderland, Matt Broadhead, and Oren Etzioni. 2007. Open information extraction from the web. In *IJCAI*.

Avrim Blum and Tom Mitchell. 1998. Combining labeled and unlabeled data with co-training. In *COLT*.

Sergey Brin. 1998. Extracting patterns and relations from the world wide web. In *WebDB Workshop at 6th International Conference on Extending Database Technology*.

Rich Caruana. 1997. Multitask learning. *Machine Learning*, 28:41–75.

Ming-Wei Chang, Lev-Arie Ratinov, and Dan Roth. 2007. Guiding semi-supervision with constraint-driven learning. In *ACL*.

Michael Collins and Yoram Singer. 1999. Unsupervised models for named entity classification. In *EMNLP*.

James R. Curran, Tara Murphy, and Bernhard Scholz. 2007. Minimising semantic drift with mutual exclusion bootstrapping. In *PACLING*.

Jeffrey Dean and Sanjay Ghemawat. 2008. Mapreduce: simplified data processing on large clusters. *Commun. ACM*, 51(1):107–113.

Doug Downey, Matthew Broadhead, and Oren Etzioni. 2007. Locating complex named entities in web text. In *IJCAI*.

Oren Etzioni, Michael Cafarella, Doug Downey, Ana-Maria Popescu, Tal Shaked, Stephen Soderland, Daniel S. Weld, and Alexander Yates. 2005. Unsupervised named-entity extraction from the web: an experimental study. *Artif. Intell.*, 165(1):91–134.

Usama M. Fayyad and Keki B. Irani. 1993. Multi-interval discretization of continuous-valued attributes for classification learning. In *UAI*.

Marti A. Hearst. 1992. Automatic acquisition of hyponyms from large text corpora. In *COLING*.

Qiuhua Liu, Xuejun Liao, and Lawrence Carin. 2008. Semi-supervised multitask learning. In *NIPS*.

David McClosky, Eugene Charniak, and Mark Johnson. 2006. Effective self-training for parsing. In *NAACL*.

Luke K. McDowell and Michael Cafarella. 2006. Ontology-driven information extraction with ontosyphon. In *ISWC*.

Metaweb Technologies. 2009. Freebase data dumps. http://download.freebase.com/datadumps/.

Marius Paşca, Dekang Lin, Jeffrey Bigham, Andrei Lifchits, and Alpa Jain. 2006. Names and similarities on the web: fact extraction in the fast lane. In *ACL*.

Marius Pasca, Dekang Lin, Jeffrey Bigham, Andrei Lifchits, and Alpa Jain. 2006. Organizing and searching the world wide web of facts - step one: The one-million fact extraction challenge. In *AAAI*.

Deepak Ravichandran and Eduard Hovy. 2002. Learning surface text patterns for a question answering system. In *ACL*.

Ellen Riloff and Rosie Jones. 1999. Learning dictionaries for information extraction by multi-level bootstrapping. In *AAAI*.

Benjamin Rosenfeld and Ronen Feldman. 2007. Using corpus statistics on entities to improve semi-supervised relation extraction from the web. In *ACL*.

Yusuke Shinyama and Satoshi Sekine. 2006. Preemptive information extraction using unrestricted relation discovery. In *HLT-NAACL*.

Mark D. Smucker, James Allan, and Ben Carterette. 2007. A comparison of statistical significance tests for information retrieval evaluation. In *CIKM*.

Sebastian Thrun. 1996. Is learning the n-th thing any easier than learning the first? In *NIPS*.

Peter D. Turney. 2001. Mining the web for synonyms: Pmi-ir versus lsa on toefl. In *EMCL*.

Nicola Ueffing. 2006. Self-training for machine translation. In *NIPS workshop on Machine Learning for Multilingual Information Access*.

Roman Yangarber. 2003. Counter-training in discovery of semantic patterns. In *ACL*.

Surrogate Learning - From Feature Independence to Semi-Supervised Classification

Sriharsha Veeramachaneni and **Ravi Kumar Kondadadi**
Thomson Reuters Research and Development
Eagan, MN 55123, USA
[harsha.veeramachaneni,ravikumar.kondadadi]@thomsonreuters.com

Abstract

We consider the task of learning a classifier from the feature space $\mathcal{X}$ to the set of classes $\mathcal{Y} = \{0, 1\}$, when the features can be partitioned into class-conditionally independent feature sets $\mathcal{X}_1$ and $\mathcal{X}_2$. We show that the class-conditional independence can be used to represent the original learning task in terms of 1) learning a classifier from $\mathcal{X}_2$ to $\mathcal{X}_1$ (in the sense of estimating the probability $P(\mathbf{x}_1|\mathbf{x}_2)$)and 2) learning the class-conditional distribution of the feature set $\mathcal{X}_1$. This fact can be exploited for semi-supervised learning because the former task can be accomplished purely from unlabeled samples. We present experimental evaluation of the idea in two real world applications.

1 Introduction

Semi-supervised learning is said to occur when the learner exploits (a presumably large quantity of) unlabeled data to supplement a relatively small labeled sample, for accurate induction. The high cost of labeled data and the simultaneous plenitude of unlabeled data in many application domains, has led to considerable interest in semi-supervised learning in recent years (Chapelle et al., 2006).

We show a somewhat surprising consequence of class-conditional feature independence that leads to a principled and easily implementable semi-supervised learning algorithm. When the feature set can be partitioned into two class-conditionally independent sets, we show that the original learning problem can be reformulated in terms of the problem of learning a first predictor from one of the partitions to the other, plus a second predictor from the latter partition to class label. That is, the latter partition acts as a *surrogate* for the class variable. Assuming that the second predictor can be learned from a relatively small labeled sample this results in an effective semi-supervised algorithm, since the first predictor can be learned from only unlabeled samples.

In the next section we present the simple yet interesting result on which our semi-supervised learning algorithm (which we call *surrogate learning*) is based. We present examples to clarify the intuition behind the approach and present a special case of our approach that is used in the applications section. We then examine related ideas in previous work and situate our algorithm among previous approaches to semi-supervised learning. We present empirical evaluation on two real world applications where the required assumptions of our algorithm are satisfied.

2 Surrogate Learning

We consider the problem of learning a classifier from the feature space $\mathcal{X}$ to the set of classes $\mathcal{Y} = \{0, 1\}$. Let the features be partitioned into $\mathcal{X} = \mathcal{X}_1 \times \mathcal{X}_2$. The random feature vector $\mathbf{x} \in \mathcal{X}$ will be represented correspondingly as $\mathbf{x} = (\mathbf{x}_1, \mathbf{x}_2)$. Since we restrict our consideration to a two-class problem, the construction of the classifier involves the estimation of the probability $P(\mathbf{y} = 0|\mathbf{x}_1, \mathbf{x}_2)$ at every point $(\mathbf{x}_1, \mathbf{x}_2) \in \mathcal{X}$.

We make the following assumptions on the joint probabilities of the classes and features.

Proceedings of the NAACL HLT Workshop on Semi-supervised Learning for Natural Language Processing, pages 10–18,
Boulder, Colorado, June 2009.

1. $P(\mathbf{x}_1, \mathbf{x}_2|\mathbf{y}) = P(\mathbf{x}_1|\mathbf{y})P(\mathbf{x}_2|\mathbf{y})$ for $\mathbf{y} \in \{0, 1\}$. That is, the feature sets $\mathbf{x}_1$ and $\mathbf{x}_2$ are class-conditionally independent for both classes. Note that, when $\mathcal{X}_1$ and $\mathcal{X}_2$ are one-dimensional, this condition is identical to the *Naive Bayes* assumption, although in general our assumption is weaker.

2. $P(\mathbf{x}_1|\mathbf{x}_2) \neq 0$, $P(\mathbf{x}_1|\mathbf{y}) \neq 0$ and $P(\mathbf{x}_1|\mathbf{y} = 0) \neq P(\mathbf{x}_1|\mathbf{y} = 1)$. These assumptions are to avoid *divide-by-zero* problems in the algebra below. If $\mathbf{x}_1$ is a discrete valued random variable and not irrelevant for the classification task, these conditions are often satisfied.

We can now show that $P(\mathbf{y} = 0|\mathbf{x}_1, \mathbf{x}_2)$ can be written as a function of $P(\mathbf{x}_1|\mathbf{x}_2)$ and $P(\mathbf{x}_1|\mathbf{y})$. When we consider the quantity $P(\mathbf{y}, \mathbf{x}_1|\mathbf{x}_2)$, we may derive the following.

$$
\begin{aligned}
& P(\mathbf{y}, \mathbf{x}_1|\mathbf{x}_2) = P(\mathbf{x}_1|\mathbf{y}, \mathbf{x}_2)P(\mathbf{y}|\mathbf{x}_2) \\
\Rightarrow\ & P(\mathbf{y}, \mathbf{x}_1|\mathbf{x}_2) = P(\mathbf{x}_1|\mathbf{y})P(\mathbf{y}|\mathbf{x}_2) \\
& \quad \text{(from the independence assumption)} \\
\Rightarrow\ & P(\mathbf{y}|\mathbf{x}_1, \mathbf{x}_2)P(\mathbf{x}_1|\mathbf{x}_2) = P(\mathbf{x}_1|\mathbf{y})P(\mathbf{y}|\mathbf{x}_2) \\
\Rightarrow\ & \frac{P(\mathbf{y}|\mathbf{x}_1, \mathbf{x}_2)P(\mathbf{x}_1|\mathbf{x}_2)}{P(\mathbf{x}_1|\mathbf{y})} = P(\mathbf{y}|\mathbf{x}_2) \qquad (1)
\end{aligned}
$$

Since $P(\mathbf{y} = 0|\mathbf{x}_2) + P(\mathbf{y} = 1|\mathbf{x}_2) = 1$, Equation 1 implies

$$
\begin{aligned}
& \frac{P(\mathbf{y} = 0|\mathbf{x}_1, \mathbf{x}_2)P(\mathbf{x}_1|\mathbf{x}_2)}{P(\mathbf{x}_1|\mathbf{y} = 0)} + \\
& \quad \frac{P(\mathbf{y} = 1|\mathbf{x}_1, \mathbf{x}_2)P(\mathbf{x}_1|\mathbf{x}_2)}{P(\mathbf{x}_1|\mathbf{y} = 1)} = 1 \\
\Rightarrow\ & \frac{P(\mathbf{y} = 0|\mathbf{x}_1, \mathbf{x}_2)P(\mathbf{x}_1|\mathbf{x}_2)}{P(\mathbf{x}_1|\mathbf{y} = 0)} + \\
& \quad \frac{(1 - P(\mathbf{y} = 0|\mathbf{x}_1, \mathbf{x}_2))\, P(\mathbf{x}_1|\mathbf{x}_2)}{P(\mathbf{x}_1|\mathbf{y} = 1)} = 1 \qquad (2)
\end{aligned}
$$

Solving Equation 2 for $P(\mathbf{y} = 0|\mathbf{x}_1, \mathbf{x}_2)$, we obtain

$$
\begin{aligned}
& P(\mathbf{y} = 0|\mathbf{x}_1, \mathbf{x}_2) = \\
& \quad \frac{P(\mathbf{x}_1|\mathbf{y} = 0)}{P(\mathbf{x}_1|\mathbf{x}_2)} \cdot \frac{P(\mathbf{x}_1|\mathbf{y} = 1) - P(\mathbf{x}_1|\mathbf{x}_2)}{P(\mathbf{x}_1|\mathbf{y} = 1) - P(\mathbf{x}_1|\mathbf{y} = 0)} \qquad (3)
\end{aligned}
$$

We have succeeded in writing $P(\mathbf{y} = 0|\mathbf{x}_1, \mathbf{x}_2)$ as a function of $P(\mathbf{x}_1|\mathbf{x}_2)$ and $P(\mathbf{x}_1|\mathbf{y})$. Although this result was previously observed in a different context by Abney in (Abney, 2002), he does not use it to derive a semi-supervised learning algorithm. This result can lead to a significant simplification of the learning task when a large amount of unlabeled data is available. The semi-supervised learning algorithm involves the following two steps.

1. From unlabeled data learn a predictor from the feature space $\mathcal{X}_2$ to the space $\mathcal{X}_1$ to predict $P(\mathbf{x}_1|\mathbf{x}_2)$. There is no restriction on the learner that can be used as long as it outputs posterior class probability estimates.

2. Estimate the quantity $P(\mathbf{x}_1|\mathbf{y})$ from a labeled samples. In case $\mathbf{x}_1$ is finite valued, this can be done by just counting. If $\mathcal{X}_1$ has low cardinality the estimation problem requires very few labeled samples. For example, if $\mathbf{x}_1$ is binary, then estimating $P(\mathbf{x}_1|\mathbf{y})$ involves estimating just two Bernoulli probabilities.

Thus, we can decouple the prediction problem into two separate tasks, one of which involves predicting $\mathbf{x}_1$ from the remaining features. In other words, $\mathbf{x}_1$ serves as a *surrogate* for the class label. Furthermore, for the two steps above there is no necessity for complete samples. The labeled examples can have the feature $\mathbf{x}_2$ missing.

At test time, an input sample $(\mathbf{x}_1, \mathbf{x}_2)$ is classified by computing $P(\mathbf{x}_1|\mathbf{y})$ and $P(\mathbf{x}_1|\mathbf{x}_2)$ from the predictors obtained from training, and plugging these values into Equation 3. Note that these two quantities are computed for the actual value of $\mathbf{x}_1$ taken by the input sample.

The following example illustrates surrogate learning.

Example 1

Consider the following variation on a problem from (Duda et al., 2000) of classifying fish on a converyor belt as either *salmon* ($\mathbf{y} = 0$) or *sea bass* ($\mathbf{y} = 1$). The features describing the fish are $\mathbf{x}_1$, a binary feature describing whether the fish is *light* ($\mathbf{x}_1 = 0$) or *dark* ($\mathbf{x}_1 = 1$), and $\mathbf{x}_2$ describes the length of the fish which is real-valued. Assume (unrealistically) that $P(\mathbf{x}_2|\mathbf{y})$, the class-conditional distribution of $\mathbf{x}_2$, the length for *salmon* is Gaussian, and for the *sea bass* is Laplacian as shown in Figure 1.

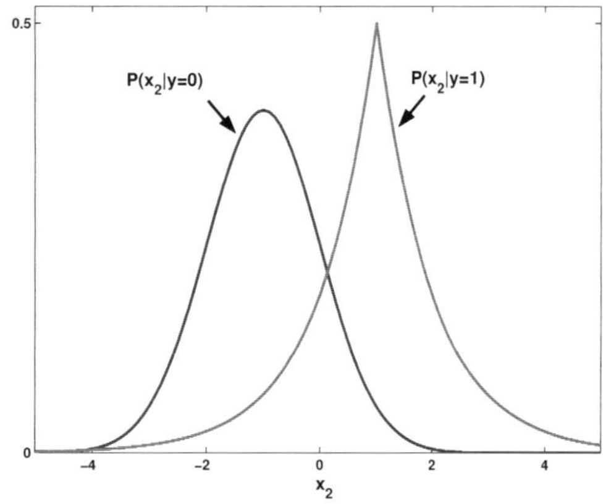

Figure 1: Class-conditional probability distributions of the feature $\mathbf{x}_2$.

Because of the class-conditional feature independence assumption, the joint distribution $P(\mathbf{x}_1, \mathbf{x}_2, \mathbf{y}) = P(\mathbf{x}_2|\mathbf{y})P(\mathbf{x}_1, \mathbf{y})$ can now be completely specified by fixing the joint probability $P(\mathbf{x}_1, \mathbf{y})$. Let $P(\mathbf{x}_1 = 0, \mathbf{y} = 0) = 0.3$, $P(\mathbf{x}_1 = 0, \mathbf{y} = 1) = 0.1$, $P(\mathbf{x}_1 = 1, \mathbf{y} = 0) = 0.2$, and $P(\mathbf{x}_1 = 1, \mathbf{y} = 1) = 0.4$. I.e., a *salmon* is more likely to be *light* than *dark* and a *sea bass* is more likely to be *dark* than *light*.

The full joint distribution is depicted in Figure 2. Also shown in Figure 2 are the conditional distributions $P(\mathbf{x}_1 = 0|\mathbf{x}_2)$ and $P(\mathbf{y} = 0|\mathbf{x}_1, \mathbf{x}_2)$.

Assume that we build a predictor to decide between $\mathbf{x}_1 =$ *light* and $\mathbf{x}_1 =$ *dark* from the *length* using a data set of unlabeled fish. On a random *salmon*, this predictor will most likely decide that $\mathbf{x}_1 =$ *light* (because, for a *salmon*, $\mathbf{x}_1 =$ *light* is more likely than $\mathbf{x}_1 =$ *dark*, and similarly for a *sea bass* the predictor often decides that $\mathbf{x}_1 =$ *dark*. Consequently the predictor provides information about the true class label $\mathbf{y}$. This can also be seen in the similarities between the curves $P(\mathbf{y} = 0|\mathbf{x}_1, \mathbf{x}_2)$ to the curve $P(\mathbf{x}_1|\mathbf{x}_2)$ in Figure 2.

Another way to interpret the example is to note that if a predictor for $P(\mathbf{x}_1|\mathbf{x}_2)$ were built on *only* the *salmons* then $P(\mathbf{x}_1 =$ *light*$|\mathbf{x}_2)$ will be a constant value (0.6). Similarly the value of $P(\mathbf{x}_1 =$ *light*$|\mathbf{x}_2)$ for *sea basses* will also be a constant value (0.2). That is, the value of $P(\mathbf{x}_1 =$ *light*$|\mathbf{x}_2)$ for a sample is a good predictor of its class. However,

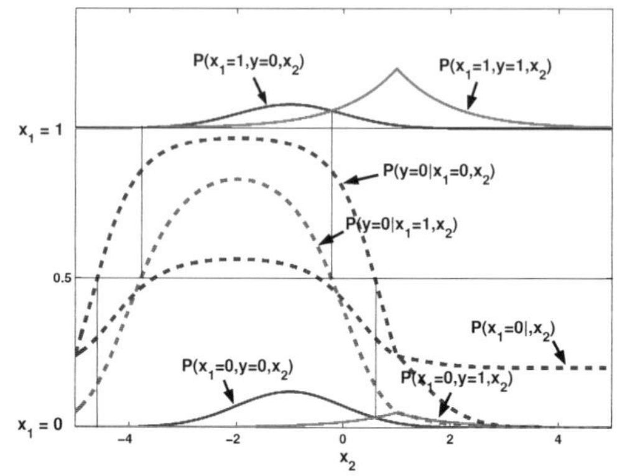

Figure 2: The joint distributions and the posterior distributions of the class $\mathbf{y}$ and the surrogate class $\mathbf{x}_1$.

surrogate learning builds the predictor $P(\mathbf{x}_1|\mathbf{x}_2)$ on unlabeled data from *both* types of fish and therefore additionally requires $P(\mathbf{x}_1|\mathbf{y})$ to estimate the boundary between the classes.

2.1 A Special Case

The independence assumptions made in the setting above may seem too strong to hold in real problems, especially because the feature sets are required to be class-conditionally independent for *both* classes. We now specialize the setting of the classification problem to the one realized in the applications we present later.

We still wish to learn a classifier from $\mathcal{X} = \mathcal{X}_1 \times \mathcal{X}_2$ to the set of classes $\mathcal{Y} = \{0, 1\}$. We make the following slightly modified assumptions.

1. $\mathbf{x}_1$ is a binary random variable. That is, $\mathcal{X}_1 = \{0, 1\}$.

2. $P(\mathbf{x}_1, \mathbf{x}_2|\mathbf{y} = 0) = P(\mathbf{x}_1|\mathbf{y} = 0)P(\mathbf{x}_2|\mathbf{y} = 0)$. We require that the feature $\mathbf{x}_1$ be class-conditionally independent of the remaining features *only* for the class $\mathbf{y} = 0$.

3. $P(\mathbf{x}_1 = 0, \mathbf{y} = 1) = 0$. This assumption says that $\mathbf{x}_1$ is a '100% recall' feature for $\mathbf{y} = 1$[1].

Assumption 3 simplifies the learning task to the estimation of the probability $P(\mathbf{y} = 0|\mathbf{x}_1 = 1, \mathbf{x}_2)$ for every point $\mathbf{x}_2 \in \mathcal{X}_2$. We can proceed as before

[1] This assumption can be seen to trivially enforce the independence of the features for class $\mathbf{y} = 1$.

to obtain the expression in Equation 3.

$$
\begin{aligned}
&P(\mathbf{y}=0|\mathbf{x}_1=1,\mathbf{x}_2) \\
&= \frac{P(\mathbf{x}_1=1|\mathbf{y}=0)}{P(\mathbf{x}_1=1|\mathbf{x}_2)}\cdots \\
&\quad\cdots\frac{P(\mathbf{x}_1=1|\mathbf{y}=1)-P(\mathbf{x}_1=1|\mathbf{x}_2)}{P(\mathbf{x}_1=1|\mathbf{y}=1)-P(\mathbf{x}_1=1|\mathbf{y}=0)} \\
&= \frac{P(\mathbf{x}_1=1|\mathbf{y}=0)}{P(\mathbf{x}_1=1|\mathbf{x}_2)}\cdot\frac{1-P(\mathbf{x}_1=1|\mathbf{x}_2)}{1-P(\mathbf{x}_1=1|\mathbf{y}=0)} \\
&= \frac{P(\mathbf{x}_1=1|\mathbf{y}=0)}{P(\mathbf{x}_1=1|\mathbf{x}_2)}\cdot\frac{P(\mathbf{x}_1=0|\mathbf{x}_2)}{P(\mathbf{x}_1=0|\mathbf{y}=0)} \\
&= \frac{P(\mathbf{x}_1=1|\mathbf{y}=0)}{P(\mathbf{x}_1=0|\mathbf{y}=0)}\cdot\frac{P(\mathbf{x}_1=0|\mathbf{x}_2)}{(1-P(\mathbf{x}_1=0|\mathbf{x}_2))}
\end{aligned}
\tag{4}
$$

Equation 4 shows that $P(\mathbf{y} = 0|\mathbf{x}_1 = 1, \mathbf{x}_2)$ is a monotonically increasing function of $P(\mathbf{x}_1 = 0|\mathbf{x}_2)$. This means that after we build a predictor from $\mathcal{X}_2$ to $\mathcal{X}_1$, we only need to establish the threshold on $P(\mathbf{x}_1 = 0|\mathbf{x}_2)$ to yield the optimum classification between $\mathbf{y} = 0$ and $\mathbf{y} = 1$. Therefore the learning proceeds as follows.

1. From unlabeled data learn a predictor from the feature space $\mathcal{X}_2$ to the binary space $\mathcal{X}_1$ to predict the quantity $P(\mathbf{x}_1|\mathbf{x}_2)$.

2. Use labeled sample to establish the threshold on $P(\mathbf{x}_1 = 0|\mathbf{x}_2)$ to achieve the desired precision-recall trade-off for the original classification problem.

Because of our assumptions, for a sample from class $\mathbf{y} = 0$ it is impossible to predict whether $\mathbf{x}_1 = 0$ or $\mathbf{x}_1 = 1$ better than random by looking at the $\mathbf{x}_2$ feature, whereas a sample from the positive class always has $\mathbf{x}_1 = 1$. Therefore the samples with $\mathbf{x}_1 = 0$ serve to delineate the positive examples among the samples with $\mathbf{x}_1 = 1$. We therefore call the samples that have $\mathbf{x}_1 = 1$ as the *target* samples and those that have $\mathbf{x}_1 = 0$ as the *background* samples.

3 Related Work

Although the idea of using unlabeled data to improve classifier accuracy has been around for several decades (Nagy and Shelton, 1966), semi-supervised learning has received much attention recently due to impressive results in some domains. The compilation of chapters edited by Chappelle et al. is an excellent introduction to the various approaches to semi-supervised learning, and the related practical and theoretical issues (Chapelle et al., 2006).

Similar to our setup, *co-training* assumes that the features can be split into two class-conditionally independent sets or 'views' (Blum and Mitchell, 1998). Also assumed is the sufficiency of either view for accurate classification. The co-training algorithm iteratively uses the unlabeled data classified with high confidence by the classifier on one view, to generate labeled data for learning the classifier on the other.

The intuition underlying co-training is that the errors caused by the classifier on one view are independent of the other view, hence can be conceived as uniform[2] noise added to the training examples for the other view. Consequently, the number of label errors in a region in the feature space is proportional to the number of samples in the region. If the former classifier is reasonably accurate, the *proportionally* distributed errors are 'washed out' by the correctly labeled examples for the latter classifier. Seeger showed that co-training can also be viewed as an instance of the Expectation-Maximization algorithm (Seeger, 2000).

The main distinction of surrogate learning from co-training is the learning of a predictor from one view to the other, as opposed to learning predictors from both views to the class label. We can therefore eliminate the requirement that both views be sufficiently informative for reasonably accurate prediction. Furthermore, unlike co-training, surrogate learning has no iterative component.

Ando and Zhang propose an algorithm to regularize the hypothesis space by simultaneously considering multiple classification tasks on the same feature space (Ando and Zhang, 2005). They then use their so-called *structural learning* algorithm for semi-supervised learning of *one* classification task, by the artificial construction of 'related' problems on unlabeled data. This is done by creating problems of predicting *observable* features of the data and learning the structural regularization parameters from these 'auxiliary' problems and unlabeled data. More recently in (Ando and Zhang, 2007) they

[2]Whether or not a label is erroneous is independent of the feature values of the latter view.

showed that, with conditionally independent feature sets predicting from one set to the other allows the construction of a feature representation that leads to an effective semi-supervised learning algorithm. Our approach directly operates on the original feature space and can be viewed another justification for the algorithm in (Ando and Zhang, 2005).

Multiple Instance Learning (MIL) is a learning setting where training data is provided as positive and negative bags of samples (Dietterich et al., 1997). A negative bag contains only negative examples whereas a positive bag contains at least one positive example. Surrogate learning can be viewed as artificially constructing a MIL problem, with the *targets* acting as one positive bag and the *backgrounds* acting as one negative bag (Section 2.1). The class-conditional feature independence assumption for class $\mathbf{y} = 0$ translates to the identical and independent distribution of the negative samples in both bags.

4 Two Applications

We applied the surrogate learning algorithm to the problems of record linkage and paraphrase generation. As we shall see, the applications satisfy the assumptions in our second (100% recall) setting.

4.1 Record Linkage/ Entity Resolution

Record linkage is the process of identification and merging of records of the same entity in different databases or the unification of records in a single database, and constitutes an important component of data management. The reader is referred to (Winkler, 1995) for an overview of the record linkage problem, strategies and systems. In natural language processing record linkage problems arise during resolution of entities found in natural language text to a gazetteer.

Our problem consisted of merging each of $\approx$ 20000 physician records, which we call the *update database*, to the record of the same physician in a *master database* of $\approx 10^6$ records. The update database has fields that are absent in the master database and *vice versa*. The fields in common include the *name* (first, last and middle initial), several *address* fields, *phone*, *specialty*, and the *year-of-graduation*. Although the *last name* and *year-of-graduation* are consistent when present, the *address*, *specialty* and *phone* fields have several inconsistencies owing to different ways of writing the address, new addresses, different terms for the same specialty, missing fields, etc. However, the *name* and *year* alone are insufficient for disambiguation. We had access to ≈ 500 manually matched update records for training and evaluation (about 40 of these update records were labeled as unmatchable due to insufficient information).

The general approach to record linkage involves two steps: 1) *blocking*, where a small set of candidate records is retrieved from the master record database, which contains the correct match with high probability, and 2) *matching*, where the fields of the update records are compared to those of the candidates for scoring and selecting the match. We performed blocking by querying the master record database with the *last name* from the update record. Matching was done by scoring a feature vector of similarities over the various fields. The feature values were either binary (verifying the equality of a particular field in the update and a master record) or continuous (some kind of normalized string edit distance between fields like *street address*, *first name* etc.).

The surrogate learning solution to our matching problem was set up as follows. We designated the binary feature of equality of *year of graduation*[3] as the '100% recall' feature $\mathbf{x}_1$, and the remaining features are relegated to $\mathbf{x}_2$. The required conditions for surrogate learning are satisfied because 1) in our data it is highly unlikely for two records with different *year- of-graduation* to belong to the same physician and 2) if it is known that the update record and a master record belong to two *different* physicians, then knowing that they have the same (or different) *year-of-graduation* provides no information about the other features. Therefore all the feature vectors with the binary feature indicating equality of *year-of-graduation* are *targets* and the remaining are *backgrounds*.

First, we used feature vectors obtained from the records in all blocks from all 20000 update records to estimate the probability $P(\mathbf{x}_1|\mathbf{x}_2)$. We used lo-

[3]We believe that the equality of the middle intial would have worked just as well for $\mathbf{x}_1$.

Table 1: Precision and Recall for record linkage.

	Training proportion	Precision	Recall
Surrogate		0.96	0.95
Supervised	0.5	0.96	0.94
Supervised	0.2	0.96	0.91

gistic regression for this prediction task. For learning the logistic regression parameters, we discarded the feature vectors for which $\mathbf{x}_1$ was missing and performed mean imputation for the missing values of other features. Second, the probability $P(\mathbf{x}_1 = 1|\mathbf{y} = 0)$ (the probability that two different randomly chosen physicians have the same year of graduation) was estimated straightforwardly from the counts of the different years-of-graduation in the master record database.

These estimates were used to assign the score $P(\mathbf{y} = 1|\mathbf{x}_1 = 1, \mathbf{x}_2)$ to the records in a block (cf. Equation 4). The score of 0 is assigned to feature vectors which have $\mathbf{x}_1 = 0$. The only caveat is calculating the score for feature vectors that had missing $\mathbf{x}_1$. For such records we assign the score $P(\mathbf{y} = 1|\mathbf{x}_2) = P(\mathbf{y} = 1|\mathbf{x}_1 = 1, \mathbf{x}_2)P(\mathbf{x}_1 = 1|\mathbf{x}_2)$. We have estimates for both quantities on the right hand side. The highest scoring record in each block was flagged as a match if it exceeded some appropriate threshold.

We compared the results of the surrogate learning approach to a supervised logistic regression based matcher which used a portion of the manual matches for training and the remaining for testing. Table 1 shows the match precision and recall for both the surrogate learning and the supervised approaches. For the supervised algorithm, we show the results for the case where half the manually matched records were used for training and half for testing, as well as for the case where a fifth of the records of training and the remaining four-fifths for testing. In the latter case, every record participated in exactly one training fold but in four test folds.

The results indicate that the surrogate learner performs better matching by exploiting the unlabeled data than the supervised learner with insufficient training data. The results although not dramatic are still promising, considering that the surrogate learning approach used *none* of the manually matched records.

4.2 Paraphrase Generation for Event Extraction

Sentence classification is often a preprocessing step for event or relation extraction from text. One of the challenges posed by sentence classification is the diversity in the language for expressing the same event or relationship. We present a surrogate learning approach to generating paraphrases for expressing the *merger-acquisition* (MA) event between two organizations in financial news. Our goal is to find paraphrase sentences for the MA event from an unlabeled corpus of news articles, that might eventually be used to train a sentence classifier that discriminates between MA and non-MA sentences.

We assume that the unlabeled sentence corpus is time-stamped and named entity tagged with organizations. We further assume that a MA sentence must mention at least two organizations. Our approach to generate paraphrases is the following. We first extract all the so-called *source* sentences from the corpus that match a few high-precision seed patterns. An example of a seed pattern used for the MA event is '<ORG1> acquired <ORG2>' (where <ORG1> and <ORG2> are place holders for strings that have been tagged as organizations). An example of a *source* sentence that matches the seed is 'It was announced yesterday that <ORG>Google Inc.<ORG> acquired <ORG>Youtube <ORG>'. The purpose of the seed patterns is to produce pairs of participant organizations in an MA event with high precision.

We then extract every sentence in the corpus that contains at least two organizations, such that at least one of them matches an organization in the *source* sentences, and has a time-stamp within a two month time window of the matching *source* sentence. Of this set of sentences, all that contain *two* or more organizations from the *same source* sentence are designated as *target* sentences, and the rest are designated as *background* sentences.

We speculate that since an organization is unlikely to have a MA relationship with two different organizations in the same time period the *backgrounds* are unlikely to contain MA sentences, and moreover the language of the non-MA *target* sentences is

Table 2: Patterns used as seeds and the number of *source* sentences matching each seed.

	Seed pattern	# of *sources*
1	<ORG> acquired <ORG>	57
2	<ORG> bought <ORG>	70
3	offer for <ORG>	287
4	to buy <ORG>	396
5	merger with <ORG>	294

indistinguishable from that of the *background* sentences. To relate the approach to surrogate learning, we note that the binary "organization-pair equality" feature (both organizations in the current sentence being the same as those in a *source* sentence) serves as the '100% recall' feature $\mathbf{x}_1$. Word unigram, bigram and trigram features were used as $\mathbf{x}_2$. This setup satisfies the required conditions for surrogate learning because 1) if a sentence is about MA, the organization pair mentioned in it must be the same as that in a *source* sentence, (i.e., if *only* one of the organizations match those in a *source* sentence, the sentence is unlikely to be about MA) and 2) if an unlabeled sentence is non-MA, then knowing whether or not it shares an organization with a *source* does not provide any information about the language in the sentence.

If the original unlabeled corpus is sufficiently large, we expect the *target* set to cover most of the paraphrases for the MA event but may contain many non-MA sentences as well. The task of generating paraphrases involves filtering the *target* sentences that are non-MA and flagging the rest of the *targets* as paraphrases. This is done by constructing a classifier between the *targets* and *backgrounds*. The feature set used for this task was a bag of word unigrams, bigrams and trigrams, generated from the sentences and selected by ranking the n-grams by the divergence of their distributions in the *targets* and *backgrounds*. A support vector machine (SVM) was used to learn to classify between the *targets* and *backgrounds* and the sentences were ranked according to the score assigned by the SVM (which is a proxy for $P(\mathbf{x}_1 = 1|\mathbf{x}_2)$). We then thresholded the score to obtain the paraphrases.

Our approach is similar in principle to the 'Snowball' system proposed in (Agichtein and Gravano, 2000) for relation extraction. Similar to us, 'Snowball' looks for known participants in a relationship in an unlabeled corpus, and uses the newly discovered contexts to extract more participant tuples. However, unlike surrogate learning, which can use a rich set of features for ranking the *targets*, 'Snowball' scores the newly extracted contexts according to a single feature value which is confidence measure based only on the number of known participant tuples that are found in the context.

Example 2 below lists some sentences to illustrate the surrogate learning approach. Note that the *targets* may contain both MA and non-MA sentences but the *backgrounds* are unlikely to be MA.

Example 2

Seed Pattern

"offer for <ORG>"

Source Sentences

1. <ORG>US Airways<ORG> said Wednesday it will increase its **offer for <ORG>Delta<ORG>**.

Target Sentences (SVM score)

1.<ORG>US Airways<ORG> were to combine with a standalone <ORG>Delta<ORG>. (1.0008563)

2.<ORG>US Airways<ORG> argued that the nearly $10 billion acquisition of <ORG>Delta<ORG> would result in an efficiently run carrier that could offer low fares to fliers. (0.99958149)

3.<ORG>US Airways<ORG> is asking <ORG>Delta<ORG>'s official creditors committee to support postponing that hearing. (-0.99914371)

Background Sentences (SVM score)

1. The cities have made various overtures to <ORG>US Airways<ORG>, including a promise from <ORG>America West Airlines<ORG> and the former <ORG>US Airways<ORG>. (0.99957752)

2. <ORG>US Airways<ORG> shares rose 8 cents to close at $53.35 on the <ORG>New York Stock Exchange<ORG>. (-0.99906444)

We tested our algorithm on an unlabeled corpus of approximately 700000 financial news articles. We experimented with the five seed patterns shown in Table 2. We extracted a total of 870 *source* sentences from the five seeds. The number of *source* sentences matching each of the seeds is also shown in Table 2. Note that the numbers add to more than 870 because it is possible for a *source* sentence to match more than one seed.

The participants that were extracted from *sources*

Table 3: Precision/Recall of surrogate learning on the MA paraphrase problem for various thresholds. The baseline of using all the *targets* as paraphrases for MA has a precision of 66% and a recall of 100%.

Threshold	Precision	Recall
0.0	0.83	0.94
-0.2	0.82	0.95
-0.8	0.79	0.99

corresponded to approximately 12000 *target* sentences and approximately 120000 *background* sentences. For the purpose of evaluation, 500 randomly selected sentences from the *targets* were manually checked leading to 330 being tagged as MA and the remaining 170 as non-MA. This corresponds to a 66% precision of the *targets*.

We then ranked the *targets* according to the score assigned by the SVM trained to classify between the *targets* and *backgrounds*, and selected all the *targets* above a threshold as paraphrases for MA. Table 3 presents the precision and recall on the 500 manually tagged sentences as the threshold varies. The results indicate that our approach provides an effective way to rank the *target* sentences according to their likelihood of being about MA.

To evaluate the capability of the method to find paraphrases, we conducted five separate experiments using each pattern in Table 2 individually as a seed and counting the number of obtained sentences containing each of the other patterns (using a threshold of 0.0). These numbers are shown in the different columns of Table 4. Although new patterns are obtained, their distribution only roughly resembles the original distribution in the corpus. We attribute this to the correlation in the language used to describe a MA event based on its type (merger vs. acquisition, hostile takeover vs. seeking a buyer, etc.).

Finally we used the paraphrases, which were found by surrogate learning, to augment the training data for a MA sentence classifier and evaluated its accuracy. We first built a SVM classifier only on a portion of the labeled *targets* and classified the remaining. This approach yielded an accuracy of 76% on the test set (with two-fold cross validation). We then added all the *targets* scored above a threshold by surrogate learning as positive examples (4000

Table 4: Number of sentences found by surrogate learning matching each of the remaining seed patterns, when only one of the patterns was used as a seed. Each column is for one experiment with the corresponding pattern used as the seed. For example, when only the first pattern was used as the seed, we obtained 18 sentences that match the fourth pattern.

Seeds	1	2	3	4	5
1		2	2	5	1
2	5		6	7	5
3	4	6		152	103
4	18	16	93		57
5	3	9	195	57	

positive sentences in all were added), and all the *backgrounds* that scored below a low threshold as negative examples (27000 sentences), to the training data and repeated the two-fold cross validation. The classifier learned on the augmented training data improved the accuracy on the test data to 86% .

We believe that better designed features (than word n-grams) will provide paraphrases with higher precision and recall of the MA sentences found by surrogate learning. To apply our approach to a new event extraction problem, the design step also involves the selection of the x_1 feature such that the *targets* and *backgrounds* satisfy our assumptions.

5 Conclusions

We presented surrogate learning – an easily implementable semi-supervised learning algorithm that can be applied when the features satisfy the required independence assumptions. We presented two applications, showed how the assumptions are satisfied, and presented empirical evidence for the efficacy of our algorithm. We have also applied surrogate learning to problems in information retrieval and document zoning. We expect that surrogate learning is sufficiently general to be applied in many NLP applications, if the features are carefully designed. We briefly note that a surrogate learning method based on regression and requiring only *mean independence* instead of full statistical independence can be derived using techniques similar to those in Section 2 – this modification is closely related to the problem and solution presented in (Quadrianto et al., 2008).

References

S. Abney. 2002. Bootstrapping. In *In Proceedings of the 40th Annual Meeting of the Association for Computational Linguistics*, pages 360–367.

E. Agichtein and L. Gravano. 2000. Snowball: Extracting Relations from Large Plain-Text Collections. In *Proceedings of the 5th ACM International Conference on Digital Libraries (ACM DL)*, pages 85–94, June, 2-7.

R. K. Ando and T. Zhang. 2005. A framework for learning predictive structures from multiple tasks and unlabeled data. *JMLR*, 6:1817–1853.

R. K. Ando and T. Zhang. 2007. Two-view feature generation model for semi-supervised learning. In *ICML*, pages 25–32.

A. Blum and T. Mitchell. 1998. Combining labeled and unlabeled data with co-training. In *COLT*, pages 92–100.

O. Chapelle, B. Schölkopf, and A. Zien, editors. 2006. *Semi-Supervised Learning*. MIT Press, Cambridge, MA.

T. G. Dietterich, R. H. Lathrop, and T. Lozano-Perez. 1997. Solving the multiple instance problem with axis-parallel rectangles. *Artificial Intelligence*, 89(1-2):31–71.

R. O. Duda, P. E. Hart, and D. G. Stork. 2000. *Pattern Classification*. Wiley-Interscience Publication.

G. Nagy and G. L. Shelton. 1966. Self-corrective character recognition system. *IEEE Trans. Information Theory*, 12(2):215–222.

N. Quadrianto, A. J. Smola, T. S. Caetano, and Q. V. Le. 2008. Estimating labels from label proportions. In *ICML '08: Proceedings of the 25th international conference on Machine learning*, pages 776–783.

M. Seeger. 2000. Input-dependent regularization of conditional density models. Technical report, Institute for ANC, Edinburgh, UK. See `http://www.dai.ed.ac.uk/~seeger/papers.html`.

W. E. Winkler. 1995. Matching and record linkage. In *Business Survey Methods*, pages 355–384. Wiley.

Keepin' It Real: Semi-Supervised Learning with Realistic Tuning

Andrew B. Goldberg
Computer Sciences Department
University of Wisconsin-Madison
Madison, WI 53706, USA
goldberg@cs.wisc.edu

Xiaojin Zhu
Computer Sciences Department
University of Wisconsin-Madison
Madison, WI 53706, USA
jerryzhu@cs.wisc.edu

Abstract

We address two critical issues involved in applying semi-supervised learning (SSL) to a real-world task: parameter tuning and choosing which (if any) SSL algorithm is best suited for the task at hand. To gain a better understanding of these issues, we carry out a medium-scale empirical study comparing supervised learning (SL) to two popular SSL algorithms on eight natural language processing tasks under three performance metrics. We simulate how a practitioner would go about tackling a new problem, including parameter tuning using cross validation (CV). We show that, under such realistic conditions, each of the SSL algorithms can be worse than SL on some datasets. However, we also show that CV can select SL/SSL to achieve "agnostic SSL," whose performance is almost always no worse than SL. While CV is often dismissed as unreliable for SSL due to the small amount of labeled data, we show that it is in fact effective for accuracy even when the labeled dataset size is as small as 10.

1 Introduction

Imagine you are a real-world practitioner working on a machine learning problem in natural language processing. If you have unlabeled data, should you use semi-supervised learning (SSL)? Which SSL algorithm should you use? How should you set its parameters? Or could it actually hurt performance, in which case you might be better off with supervised learning (SL)?

A large number of SSL algorithms have been developed in recent years that allow one to improve performance with unlabeled data, in tasks such as text classification, sequence labeling, and parsing (Zhu, 2005; Chapelle et al., 2006; Brefeld and Scheffer, 2006). However, many of them are tested on "SSL-friendly" datasets, such as "two moons," USPS, and MNIST. Furthermore, the algorithms' parameters are often chosen based on test set performance or manually set based on heuristics and researcher experience. These issues create practical concerns for deploying SSL in the real world.

We note that (Chapelle et al., 2006)'s benchmark chapter explores these issues to some extent by comparing several SSL methods on several real and artificial datasets. The authors reach the conclusions that parameter tuning is difficult with little labeled data and that no method is universally superior. We reexamine these issues in the context of NLP tasks and offer a simple attempt at overcoming these roadblocks to practical application of SSL.

The contributions of this paper include:

- We present a medium-scale empirical study comparing SL to two popular SSL algorithms on eight less-familiar tasks using three performance metrics. Importantly, we *tune parameters realistically* based on cross validation (CV), as a practitioner would do in reality.
- We show that, under such realistic conditions, each of the SSL algorithms can be worse than SL on some datasets.
- However, this can be prevented. We show that CV can be used to select SL/SSL to achieve *agnostic SSL*, whose performance is almost always no worse than SL. Traditionally, CV is

Proceedings of the NAACL HLT Workshop on Semi-supervised Learning for Natural Language Processing, pages 19–27,
Boulder, Colorado, June 2009.

often dismissed as unreliable for SSL because of the small labeled dataset size. But we show that CV is effective when using accuracy as an optimization criterion, even when the labeled dataset size is as small as 10.

- We show the power of cloud computing: we were able to complete roughly 3 months worth of experiments in less than a week.

2 SSL with Realistic Tuning

Given a particular labeled and unlabeled dataset, how should you set parameters for a particular SSL model? The most realistic approach for a practitioner is to use CV to tune parameters on a grid. We therefore argue that the model parameters obtained in this way truly determine how SSL will perform in practice. Algorithm 1 describes a particular instance[1] of CV in detail. We call it "RealSSL," as this is all a real user can hope to do when applying SSL (and SL too) in a realistic problem scenario.

3 Experimental Procedure

Given the RealSSL procedure in Algorithm 1, we designed an experimental setup to simulate different settings that a real-world practitioner might face when given a new task and a set of algorithms to choose from (some of which use unlabeled data). This will allow us to compare algorithms across datasets in a variety of situations. Algorithm 2 measures the performance of one algorithm on one dataset for several different l and u combinations. Specifically, we consider $l \in \{10, 100\}$ and $u \in \{100, 1000\}$. For each combination, we perform multiple trials ($T = 10$ here) using different random assignments of data to $D_{labeled}$ and $D_{unlabeled}$, to obtain confidence intervals around our performance measurements. All random selections of subsets of data are the same across different algorithms' runs, to permit paired t-tests for evaluation. Note that, when $l \neq \max(L)$ or $u \neq \max(U)$, a portion of D_{pool} is not used for training. Also, the RealSSL procedure ensures that all parameters are tuned by cross-validation without ever seeing the held-out test set D_{test}. Lastly, we stress that the same grid of algorithm-specific parameter values (discussed in Section 5) is considered for all datasets.

[1]The particular choice of 5-fold CV, the way to split labeled and unlabeled data, and the parameter grid, is important too. But we view them as secondary to the fact that we are tuning SSL by CV.

4 Datasets

Table 1 summarizes the datasets used for the comparisons. In this study we consider only binary classification tasks. Note that d is the number of dimensions, $P(y = 1)$ is the proportion of instances in the full dataset belonging to class $y = 1$, and $|D_{test}|$ refers to the size of the test set (the instances remaining after $\max(L) + \max(U) = 1100$ have been set aside for training trials).

[MacWin] is the Mac versus Windows text classification data from the 20-newsgroups dataset, preprocessed by the authors of (Sindhwani et al., 2005).

[Interest] is a binary version of the word sense disambiguation data from (Bruce and Wiebe, 1994). The task is to distinguish the sense of "interest" meaning "money paid for the use of money" from the other five senses (e.g., "readiness to give attention," "a share in a company or business"). The data comes from a corpus of part-of-speech (POS) tagged sentences containing the word "interest." Each instance is a bag-of-word/POS vector, excluding words containing the root "interest" and those that appeared in less than three sentences overall.

Datasets [aut-avn] and [real-sim] are the auto/aviation and real/simulated text classification datasets from the SRAA corpus of UseNet articles. The [ccat] and [gcat] datasets involve identifying corporate and government articles, respectively, in the RCV1 corpus. We use the versions of these datasets prepared by the authors of (Sindhwani et al., 2006).

Finally, the two WISH datasets come from (Goldberg et al., 2009) and involve discriminating between sentences that contain wishful expressions and those that do not. The instances in [WISH-politics] correspond to sentences taken from a political discussion board, while [WISH-products] is based on sentences from Amazon product reviews. The features are a combination of word and template features as described in (Goldberg et al., 2009).

Input: dataset $D_{labeled} = \{x_i, y_i\}_{i=1}^{l}$, $D_{unlabeled} = \{x_j\}_{j=1}^{u}$, $algorithm$, performance $metric$

Randomly partition $D_{labeled}$ into 5 equally-sized disjoint subsets $\{D_{l1}, D_{l2}, D_{l3}, D_{l4}, D_{l5}\}$.
Randomly partition $D_{unlabeled}$ into 5 equally-sized disjoint subsets $\{D_{u1}, D_{u2}, D_{u3}, D_{u4}, D_{u5}\}$.
Combine partitions: Let $D_{fold\ k} = D_{lk} \cup D_{uk}$ for all $k = 1, \ldots, 5$.
foreach *parameter configuration in grid* **do**
    foreach *fold k* **do**
        Train model using $algorithm$ on $\cup_{i \neq k} D_{fold\ i}$.
        Evaluate $metric$ on $D_{fold\ k}$.
    end
    Compute the average $metric$ value across the 5 folds.
end
Choose parameter configuration that optimizes average $metric$.
Train model using $algorithm$ and the chosen parameters on $D_{labeled}$ and $D_{unlabeled}$.

Output: Optimal model; Average $metric$ value achieved by optimal parameters during tuning.

Algorithm 1: RealSSL procedure for running an SSL (or SL, simply ignore the unlabeled data) algorithm on a specific labeled and unlabeled dataset using cross-validation to tune parameters.

Input: dataset $D = \{x_i, y_i\}_{i=1}^{n}$, $algorithm$, performance $metric$, set L, set U, trials T
Randomly divide D into D_{pool} (of size $\max(L) + \max(U)$) and D_{test} (the rest).
foreach *l in L* **do**
    foreach *u in U* **do**
        foreach *trial 1 up to T* **do**
            Randomly select $D_{labeled} = \{x_j, y_j\}_{j=l}^{l}$ and $D_{unlabeled} = \{x_k\}_{k=1}^{u}$ from D_{pool}.
            Run RealSSL($D_{labeled}$, $D_{unlabeled}$, $algorithm$, $metric$) to obtain model and tuning performance value (see Algorithm 1).
            Use model to classify $D_{unlabeled}$ and record transductive $metric$ value.
            Use model to classify D_{test} and record test $metric$ value.
        end
    end
end
Output: Tuning, transductive, and test performance for T runs of $algorithm$ using all l and u combinations.

Algorithm 2: Experimental procedure used for all comparisons.

Name	d	$P(y=1)$	$\|D_{test}\|$
[MacWin]	7511	0.51	846
[Interest]	2687	0.53	1268
[aut-avn]	20707	0.65	70075
[real-sim]	20958	0.31	71209
[ccat]	47236	0.47	22019
[gcat]	47236	0.30	22019
[WISH-politics]	13610	0.34	4999
[WISH-products]	4823	0.12	129

Table 1: Datasets used in benchmark comparison. See text for details.

5 Algorithms

We consider only linear classifiers for this study, since they tend to work well for text problems. In future work, we plan to explore a range of kernels and other non-linear classifiers.

As a baseline supervised learning method, we use a support vector machine (SVM), as implemented by SVM^{light} (Joachims, 1999). This baseline simply ignores all the unlabeled data $(\mathbf{x}_{l+1}, \ldots, \mathbf{x}_n)$. Recall this solves the following regularized risk minimization problem

$$\min_f \frac{1}{2}||f||_2^2 + C\sum_{i=1}^{l}\max(0, 1 - y_i f(\mathbf{x}_i)), \quad (1)$$

where $f(\mathbf{x}) = \mathbf{w}^\top\mathbf{x} + b$, and C is a parameter controlling the trade-off between training errors and model complexity. Using the procedure outlined above, we tune C over a grid of values $\{10^{-6}, 10^{-5}, 10^{-4}, 10^{-3}, 10^{-2}, 10^{-1}, 1, 10, 100\}$.

We consider two popular SSL algorithms, which make different assumptions about the link between the marginal data distribution $\mathcal{P}_x$ and the conditional label distribution $\mathcal{P}_{y|x}$. If the assumption does not hold in a particular dataset, the SSL algorithm could use the unlabeled data "incorrectly," and perform worse than SL.

The first SSL algorithm we use is a semi-supervised support vector machine (S3VM), which makes the cluster assumption: the classes are well-separated clusters of data, such that the decision boundary falls into a low density region in the feature space. While many implementations exist, we chose the deterministic annealing (DA) algorithm implemented in the SVMlin package (Sindhwani et al., 2006; Sindhwani and Keerthi, 2007). This DA algorithm often achieved the best accuracy across several datasets in the empirical comparison in (Sindhwani and Keerthi, 2007), despite being slower than the multi-switch algorithm presented in the same paper. Note that the transductive SVM implemented in SVM^{light} would have been prohibitively slow to carry out the range of experiments conducted here. Recall that an S3VM seeks an optimal classifier f^* that cuts through a region of low density between clusters of data. One way to view this is that it tries to find the best possible labeling of the unlabeled data such the classifier maximizes the margin on both labeled and unlabeled data points. This is achieved by solving the following non-convex minimization problem

$$\min_{f, \mathbf{y}' \in \{-1,1\}^u} \frac{\lambda}{2}||f||_2^2 + \frac{1}{l}\sum_{i=1}^{l} V(y_i f(\mathbf{x}_i) + \frac{\lambda'}{u}\sum_{j=l+1}^{n} V(y'_j f(\mathbf{x}_j)),$$

subject to a class-balance constraint. Note that V is a loss function (typically the hinge loss as in (1)), and the parameters λ, λ' control the relative importance of model complexity versus locating a low-density region within the unlabeled data. We tune both parameters in a grid of values $\{10^{-6}, 10^{-5}, 10^{-4}, 10^{-3}, 10^{-2}, 10^{-1}, 1, 10, 100\}$. In past studies (Sindhwani et al., 2006), λ was set to 1, and λ' was tuned over a grid containing a subset of these values.

Finally, as an example of a graph-based SSL method, we consider manifold regularization (MR) (Belkin et al., 2006), using the implementation provided on the authors' Web site.[2] This algorithm makes the manifold assumption: the labels are "smooth" with respect to a graph connecting labeled and unlabeled instances. In other words, if two instances are connected by a strong edge (e.g., they are highly similar to one another), their labels tend to be the same. Manifold regularization represents a family of methods; we specifically use the Laplacian SVM, which extends the basic SVM optimization

[2] http://manifold.cs.uchicago.edu/manifold_regularization/software.html

problem with a graph-based regularization term.

$$\min_f \gamma_A ||f||_2^2 + \frac{1}{l}\sum_{i=1}^{l} \max(0, 1 - y_i f(\mathbf{x}_i))$$
$$+ \gamma_I \sum_{i=1}^{n}\sum_{j=1}^{n} w_{ij}(f(\mathbf{x}_i) - f(\mathbf{x}_j))^2,$$

where γ_A and γ_I are parameters that trade off ambient and intrinsic smoothness, and w_{ij} is a graph weight between instances $\mathbf{x}_i$ and $\mathbf{x}_j$. In this paper, we consider kNN graphs with $k \in \{3, 10, 20\}$. Edge weights are formed using a heat kernel $w_{ij} = \exp(-\frac{||\mathbf{x}_i - \mathbf{x}_j||^2}{2\sigma^2})$, where σ is set to be the mean distance between nearest neighbors in the graph, as in (Chapelle et al., 2006). The γ parameters are each tuned over the grid $\{10^{-6}, 10^{-4}, 10^{-2}, 1, 100\}$.

Of course, many other SSL algorithms exist, some of which combine different assumptions (Chapelle and Zien, 2005; Karlen et al., 2008), and others which exploit multiple (real or artificial) views of the data (Blum and Mitchell, 1998; Sindhwani and Rosenberg, 2008). We plan to extend our study to include many more diverse SSL algorithms in the future.

6 Choosing an Algorithm for a Real-World Task

Given the choice of several algorithms, how should one choose the best one to apply to a particular learning setting? Traditionally, CV is used for model selection in supervised learning settings. However, with only a small amount of labeled data in semi-supervised settings, model selection with CV is often viewed as unreliable. We explicitly tested this hypothesis by using CV to not only choose the parameters of the model, but also choose the type of model itself. The main goal is to automatically choose between SVM, S3VM, and MR for a particular learning setting, in an attempt to ensure that the final performance is never hurt by including unlabeled data (which might be called agnostic SSL).

Given a set of algorithms (e.g., one SL, several SSL), the procedure is the following:

1. Tune the parameters of each algorithm on the labeled and unlabeled training set using Algorithm 1.[3]

2. Compare the best tuning performance (5-fold CV average) achieved by the optimal parameters for each of the algorithms.

   - If there are no ties, select the algorithm with the highest tuning performance.
   - If there is a tie, and SL is among the best, select SL.
   - If there is a tie between SSL algorithms, select one of them at random.

3. Use the selected "Best Tuning" algorithm (and the tuned parameters) to build a model on all the training data; then apply it to the test data.

Note that the procedure is conservative in that it prefers SL in the case of ties. In this paper, we use this simple "best tuning performance" heuristic.

Finally, we stress the fact that, when applying this procedure within the context of Algorithm 2, a potentially different algorithm is chosen in each of the 10 trials for a particular setting. This simulates the real-world scenario where one only has a single fixed training set of labeled and unlabeled data and must choose a single algorithm to produce a model for future predictions.

7 Performance Metrics

We compare different algorithms' performance using three metrics often used for evaluation in NLP tasks: accuracy, maxF1, and AUROC. Accuracy is simply the fraction of instances correctly classified. MaxF1 is the maximal F1 value (harmonic mean of recall and precision) achieved over the entire precision-recall curve (Cai and Hofmann, 2003). AUROC is the area under the ROC curve (Fawcett, 2004). Throughout the paper, when we discuss a result involving a particular metric, the algorithms use this metric as the criterion for parameter tuning, and we use it for the final evaluation. We are not simply evaluating a single experiment using multiple metrics—the experiments are fundamentally different and produce different learned models.

[3] We ensure each algorithm uses the same 5 partitions during the tuning step.

8 Results

We now report the results of our empirical comparison of SL and SSL on the eight NLP datasets. We first consider each dataset separately and examine how often each type of algorithm outperforms the other. We then examine cross-dataset performance.

8.1 Detailed Results

Table 2 contains all results for SVM, S3VM, and MR for all datasets and all metrics.[4] Note that within each l,u cell for a particular dataset and evaluation metric, we show the maximum value in each row (tune, transductive, or test) in boldface. Results that are not statistically significantly different using a paired t-test are also shown in boldface.

Several things are immediately obvious from Table 2. First, no algorithm is superior in all datasets or settings. In several cases, all algorithms are statistically indistinguishable. Most importantly, though, each of the SSL algorithms can be worse than SL on some datasets using some metric. We used paired t-tests to compare transductive and test performance of each SSL algorithm with SVM for a particular l,u combination and dataset (32 settings total per evaluation metric). In terms of accuracy, MR transductive performance is significantly worse than SVM in 5 settings, while MR test performance is significantly worse in 7 settings. MR is also significantly worse in 4 settings based on transductive maxF1, in 3 settings based on transductive AUROC, and 1 setting based on test AUROC. S3VM is significantly worse than SVM in 2 settings based on transductive maxF1, 2 settings based on transductive AUROC, and in 1 setting based on test AUROC. While these numbers may seem relatively low, it is important to realize that each algorithm may be worse than SSL many times on a trial-by-trial basis, which is the more realistic scenario: a practitioner has only a single dataset to work with. Results based on individual trials are discussed below shortly.

[4]Note that the results here for a particular dataset and algorithm combination may be qualitatively and quantitatively different than in previous published work, due to differences in parameter tuning, choices of parameter grids, l and u sizes, and randomization. We are not trying to replicate or raise doubt about past results: we simply intend to compare algorithms on a wide array of datasets using the standardized procedures outlined above.

We also applied our "Best Tuning" model selection procedure to automatically choose a single algorithm for each trial in each setting. We compare average SL test performance versus the average test performance of the Best Tuning selections across the 10 trials (not shown in Table 2). Comparisons based on transductive performance are similar. When the performance metric is test accuracy, the Best Tuning algorithm performs statistically significantly better than SL in 24 settings and worse in only 6 settings. In the remaining 2 settings, Best Tuning chose SL in all 10 trials, so they are equivalent. These results suggest that accuracy-based tuning is a valid method for choosing a SSL algorithm to improve accuracy on test data. To some extent, this holds for maxF1, too: the Best Tuning selections perform better than SL (on average) in 18 settings and worse in 14 settings when tuning and test evaluation is based on maxF1. However, when using AUROC as the performance metric, cross validation seems to be unreliable: Best Tuning produces a better result in only 11 out of the 32 settings.

8.2 Results Aggregated Across Datasets

We now aggregate the detailed results to better understand the relative performance of the different methods across all datasets. We perform this summary evaluation in two ways, based on test set performance (transductive performance is similar). First, we compare the SSL algorithms across all datasets based on the numbers of times each is worse than, the same as, or better than SL. For each of the 80 trials of a particular l,u,metric combination, we compare the performance of S3VM, MR, and Best Tuning to SVM. Note that each of these comparisons is akin to a real-world scenario where a practitioner would have to choose an algorithm to use. Table 3 lists tuples of the form "(#trials worse than SVM, #trials equal to SVM, #trials better than SVM)." Note that the numbers in each tuple sum to 80. The perfect SSL algorithm would have a tuple of "(0, 0, 80)," meaning that it always outperforms SL. In terms of accuracy (Table 3, top) and maxF1 (Table 3, middle), the Best Tuning method turns out to do worse than SVM less often than either S3VM or MR does (i.e., the first number in the tuples for Best Tuning is lower than the corresponding numbers for the other algorithms). At the same time, Best Tuning

		accuracy						maxF1						AUROC						
		$u = 100$			$u = 1000$			$u = 100$			$u = 1000$			$u = 100$			$u = 1000$			
Dataset	l	SVM	S3VM	MR	SVM	S3VM	MR	SVM	S3VM	MR	SVM	S3VM	MR	SVM	S3VM	MR	SVM	S3VM	MR	
[MacWin]	10	0.60	**0.72**	**0.83**	0.60	0.72	**0.86**	**0.66**	**0.67**	**0.67**	**0.66**	**0.67**	**0.67**	**0.63**	**0.69**	**0.67**	**0.63**	**0.69**	**0.69**	Tune
		0.51	0.51	**0.70**	0.51	0.50	**0.69**	0.74	**0.77**	**0.80**	**0.74**	**0.74**	**0.75**	0.72	**0.75**	**0.82**	0.72	**0.71**	**0.80**	Trans
		0.53	0.50	**0.71**	0.53	0.50	**0.68**	0.74	0.75	**0.79**	**0.74**	**0.75**	**0.74**	0.73	**0.72**	**0.83**	**0.73**	**0.71**	**0.76**	Test
	100	0.87	0.87	**0.91**	0.87	0.87	**0.90**	**0.94**	**0.95**	**0.95**	**0.94**	**0.95**	**0.95**	0.96	**0.97**	**0.97**	**0.96**	**0.96**	**0.96**	Tune
		0.89	**0.89**	**0.89**	**0.89**	**0.89**	**0.89**	0.91	**0.93**	**0.92**	**0.91**	**0.90**	**0.90**	**0.97**	**0.97**	**0.96**	**0.97**	**0.97**	0.96	Trans
		0.89	0.89	**0.91**	**0.89**	**0.89**	**0.90**	**0.92**	**0.92**	**0.92**	**0.92**	**0.91**	**0.91**	**0.97**	**0.97**	**0.97**	**0.97**	**0.97**	0.97	Test
[Interest]	10	**0.68**	**0.75**	**0.78**	0.68	**0.75**	**0.79**	0.73	**0.77**	**0.77**	0.73	**0.78**	**0.77**	0.52	**0.66**	**0.66**	0.52	**0.68**	**0.64**	Tune
		0.52	**0.56**	**0.56**	**0.52**	**0.56**	**0.56**	**0.72**	**0.72**	**0.72**	**0.72**	**0.71**	**0.71**	**0.55**	**0.54**	**0.54**	0.55	**0.56**	**0.61**	Trans
		0.52	**0.57**	**0.57**	0.52	**0.57**	**0.58**	**0.68**	**0.69**	**0.69**	**0.68**	**0.69**	**0.69**	**0.58**	**0.56**	**0.61**	0.58	**0.58**	**0.62**	Test
	100	0.77	**0.78**	0.76	0.77	**0.78**	**0.77**	0.84	**0.85**	**0.85**	0.84	**0.85**	0.84	0.89	**0.90**	0.89	**0.89**	**0.85**	**0.84**	Tune
		0.79	**0.79**	0.71	**0.79**	**0.79**	**0.77**	**0.84**	**0.83**	0.82	**0.84**	0.81	0.81	**0.91**	**0.91**	**0.89**	**0.91**	0.79	0.87	Trans
		0.81	**0.80**	0.78	**0.81**	**0.80**	0.79	**0.82**	**0.81**	**0.81**	**0.82**	**0.81**	**0.81**	**0.90**	**0.91**	**0.89**	**0.90**	**0.81**	0.88	Test
[aut-avn]	10	**0.72**	**0.76**	**0.82**	**0.72**	**0.76**	**0.79**	**0.89**	**0.92**	**0.91**	**0.89**	**0.92**	**0.91**	**0.58**	**0.67**	**0.65**	**0.58**	**0.67**	**0.65**	Tune
		0.65	**0.63**	**0.67**	**0.65**	**0.61**	**0.69**	**0.83**	**0.83**	**0.84**	**0.83**	**0.81**	**0.82**	**0.71**	**0.67**	**0.73**	**0.71**	**0.65**	**0.72**	Trans
		0.62	**0.61**	**0.67**	**0.62**	**0.61**	**0.67**	0.80	**0.81**	**0.82**	**0.80**	**0.81**	**0.81**	**0.71**	**0.70**	**0.73**	**0.71**	**0.65**	**0.69**	Test
	100	0.75	0.82	**0.87**	0.75	0.82	**0.86**	0.94	**0.94**	**0.95**	**0.94**	**0.94**	**0.94**	0.93	**0.94**	**0.94**	0.93	**0.94**	0.93	Tune
		0.77	0.79	**0.88**	0.77	0.83	**0.87**	**0.92**	**0.92**	**0.91**	**0.92**	**0.91**	**0.90**	**0.93**	**0.93**	0.91	**0.93**	**0.94**	**0.93**	Trans
		0.77	0.82	**0.89**	0.77	0.83	**0.87**	**0.91**	**0.91**	**0.91**	**0.91**	**0.91**	**0.91**	**0.95**	**0.94**	**0.95**	**0.95**	**0.95**	**0.95**	Test
[real-sim]	10	0.53	0.63	**0.82**	0.53	0.63	**0.78**	**0.65**	**0.66**	**0.66**	**0.65**	**0.66**	**0.65**	**0.77**	**0.81**	**0.81**	**0.77**	**0.81**	**0.77**	Tune
		0.64	0.63	**0.72**	**0.64**	**0.64**	**0.70**	0.57	**0.66**	**0.70**	0.57	**0.62**	**0.56**	0.65	**0.75**	**0.79**	**0.65**	**0.74**	**0.67**	Trans
		0.65	**0.66**	**0.74**	**0.65**	**0.66**	**0.68**	0.53	0.58	**0.63**	0.53	**0.59**	**0.53**	0.64	**0.73**	**0.80**	**0.64**	**0.74**	**0.66**	Test
	100	0.74	0.73	**0.86**	0.74	0.73	**0.84**	0.88	**0.90**	**0.90**	0.88	**0.91**	0.89	0.93	**0.94**	**0.94**	0.93	**0.94**	0.93	Tune
		0.78	0.76	**0.84**	0.78	0.78	**0.85**	**0.81**	**0.83**	**0.79**	**0.81**	**0.81**	**0.81**	**0.94**	**0.93**	**0.91**	**0.94**	**0.94**	0.94	Trans
		0.79	0.78	**0.85**	0.79	0.78	**0.85**	0.78	**0.79**	**0.78**	0.78	**0.79**	0.79	**0.93**	**0.93**	**0.93**	0.93	**0.94**	0.93	Test
[ccat]	10	0.54	0.60	**0.82**	0.54	0.60	**0.81**	**0.84**	**0.85**	**0.85**	**0.84**	**0.85**	**0.84**	**0.74**	**0.78**	**0.78**	**0.74**	**0.78**	**0.74**	Tune
		0.50	0.49	**0.65**	0.50	0.51	**0.67**	**0.69**	**0.69**	**0.73**	**0.69**	0.67	**0.69**	**0.60**	**0.61**	**0.71**	0.60	**0.59**	**0.72**	Trans
		0.49	0.52	**0.64**	0.49	0.52	**0.66**	0.66	0.66	**0.69**	**0.66**	**0.67**	**0.67**	**0.61**	**0.63**	**0.72**	**0.61**	**0.59**	**0.71**	Test
	100	0.80	0.80	**0.84**	0.80	0.80	**0.84**	**0.89**	**0.89**	**0.90**	**0.89**	**0.89**	**0.89**	**0.91**	**0.92**	**0.92**	**0.91**	**0.92**	**0.91**	Tune
		0.80	**0.79**	**0.80**	**0.80**	0.81	**0.83**	**0.83**	**0.85**	**0.84**	**0.83**	**0.82**	**0.82**	**0.91**	0.91	0.89	**0.91**	**0.90**	**0.91**	Trans
		0.81	**0.80**	**0.81**	**0.81**	**0.80**	**0.82**	**0.80**	**0.81**	**0.81**	**0.80**	**0.81**	**0.81**	**0.90**	0.90	**0.90**	**0.90**	**0.90**	**0.90**	Test
[gcat]	10	0.74	**0.83**	**0.82**	**0.74**	**0.79**	**0.81**	**0.44**	**0.47**	**0.46**	**0.44**	**0.47**	**0.46**	**0.69**	**0.79**	**0.75**	**0.69**	**0.79**	**0.75**	Tune
		0.69	**0.68**	**0.75**	**0.69**	**0.72**	**0.76**	0.60	**0.62**	**0.69**	**0.60**	**0.59**	**0.62**	0.71	**0.73**	**0.82**	**0.71**	**0.69**	**0.76**	Trans
		0.66	**0.67**	**0.73**	**0.66**	**0.71**	**0.74**	0.58	**0.61**	**0.66**	**0.58**	**0.60**	**0.59**	0.69	**0.69**	**0.81**	**0.69**	**0.69**	**0.75**	Test
	100	0.77	0.77	**0.90**	0.77	0.77	**0.91**	**0.92**	**0.92**	**0.93**	**0.92**	**0.92**	**0.92**	**0.97**	0.96	**0.97**	**0.97**	**0.96**	**0.96**	Tune
		0.81	0.80	**0.89**	0.81	0.81	**0.90**	**0.88**	**0.88**	0.84	**0.88**	**0.86**	**0.85**	**0.96**	**0.97**	**0.95**	**0.96**	**0.96**	**0.96**	Trans
		0.80	0.80	**0.89**	0.80	0.80	**0.90**	**0.86**	**0.86**	**0.85**	**0.86**	**0.86**	**0.86**	**0.96**	**0.96**	**0.96**	**0.96**	**0.96**	**0.96**	Test
[WISH-politics]	10	**0.70**	**0.77**	**0.79**	**0.70**	**0.77**	**0.82**	**0.61**	**0.62**	**0.61**	**0.61**	**0.62**	**0.61**	**0.74**	**0.78**	**0.74**	**0.74**	**0.78**	**0.76**	Tune
		0.50	**0.56**	**0.63**	**0.50**	**0.62**	**0.56**	**0.58**	**0.58**	**0.61**	**0.58**	**0.55**	**0.53**	0.62	**0.62**	**0.69**	**0.62**	**0.62**	**0.61**	Trans
		0.52	**0.56**	**0.60**	**0.52**	**0.62**	**0.53**	0.52	**0.53**	**0.53**	0.52	**0.54**	**0.52**	**0.57**	**0.58**	**0.61**	**0.57**	**0.62**	**0.60**	Test
	100	**0.75**	**0.75**	**0.75**	**0.75**	**0.75**	**0.74**	0.74	**0.75**	**0.76**	**0.74**	**0.75**	**0.75**	**0.79**	**0.80**	**0.80**	**0.79**	**0.80**	**0.80**	Tune
		0.73	**0.73**	**0.71**	**0.73**	**0.73**	**0.70**	**0.65**	**0.66**	**0.67**	**0.65**	**0.64**	**0.64**	**0.76**	**0.74**	**0.75**	**0.76**	**0.75**	**0.76**	Trans
		0.75	**0.75**	0.72	**0.75**	**0.75**	0.71	**0.64**	**0.63**	**0.63**	**0.64**	**0.63**	**0.64**	**0.78**	**0.76**	**0.77**	**0.78**	**0.76**	**0.77**	Test
[WISH-products]	10	**0.89**	**0.89**	0.67	**0.89**	**0.89**	0.67	0.19	**0.22**	0.16	0.19	**0.22**	0.16	**0.76**	**0.80**	**0.74**	**0.76**	**0.80**	**0.74**	Tune
		0.87	**0.87**	0.66	**0.87**	**0.87**	0.61	**0.31**	**0.29**	**0.32**	**0.31**	0.24	0.25	**0.56**	0.52	**0.58**	**0.56**	**0.54**	**0.56**	Trans
		0.90	**0.90**	0.67	**0.90**	**0.90**	0.61	0.22	0.23	**0.30**	0.22	**0.24**	**0.27**	0.50	0.53	**0.62**	0.50	**0.54**	**0.59**	Test
	100	**0.90**	**0.90**	0.82	**0.90**	**0.90**	0.81	0.49	**0.50**	**0.54**	0.49	**0.52**	**0.52**	0.73	0.73	**0.77**	**0.73**	**0.78**	**0.75**	Tune
		0.88	**0.88**	0.81	**0.88**	**0.88**	0.80	**0.34**	0.28	**0.37**	**0.34**	**0.27**	**0.30**	**0.60**	**0.55**	**0.57**	**0.60**	**0.57**	**0.61**	Trans
		0.90	**0.90**	0.79	**0.90**	**0.91**	0.76	**0.33**	**0.28**	**0.33**	**0.33**	**0.32**	**0.38**	**0.59**	**0.56**	**0.60**	**0.59**	**0.56**	**0.60**	Test

Table 2: Benchmark comparison results. All numbers are averages over 10 trials. Within each cell of nine numbers, the boldface indicates the maximum value in each row, as well as others in the row that are not statistically significantly different based on a paired t-test.

		$u = 100$			$u = 1000$			
Metric	l	S3VM	MR	Best Tuning	S3VM	MR	Best Tuning	
accuracy	10	(14, 27, 39)	(27, 0, 53)	(8, 31, 41)	(14, 25, 41)	(27, 0, 53)	(8, 29, 43)	Test
	100	(27, 7, 46)	(38, 0, 42)	(20, 16, 44)	(27, 6, 47)	(37, 0, 43)	(16, 19, 45)	Test

Metric	l	S3VM	MR	Best Tuning	S3VM	MR	Best Tuning	
maxF1	10	(29, 2, 49)	(16, 1, 63)	(14, 55, 11)	(27, 0, 53)	(24, 0, 56)	(13, 53, 14)	Test
	100	(39, 0, 41)	(34, 4, 42)	(31, 15, 34)	(39, 1, 40)	(44, 4, 32)	(26, 21, 33)	Test

Metric	l	S3VM	MR	Best Tuning	S3VM	MR	Best Tuning	
AUROC	10	(26, 0, 54)	(11, 0, 69)	(12, 57, 11)	(25, 0, 55)	(25, 0, 55)	(11, 56, 13)	Test
	100	(43, 0, 37)	(37, 0, 43)	(38, 8, 34)	(38, 0, 42)	(46, 0, 34)	(28, 24, 28)	Test

Table 3: Aggregate test performance comparisons versus SVM in 80 trials per setting. Each cell contains a tuple of the form "(#trials worse than SVM, #trials equal to SVM, #trials better than SVM)."

		$u = 100$				$u = 1000$				
Metric	l	SVM	S3VM	MR	Best Tuning	SVM	S3VM	MR	Best Tuning	
accuracy	10	0.61	0.62	0.67	0.68	0.61	0.63	0.64	0.67	Test
	100	0.81	0.82	0.83	0.85	0.81	0.82	0.83	0.85	Test

Metric	l	SVM	S3VM	MR	Best Tuning	SVM	S3VM	MR	Best Tuning	
maxF1	10	0.59	0.61	0.64	0.59	0.59	0.61	0.61	0.59	Test
	100	0.76	0.75	0.76	0.75	0.76	0.76	0.76	0.76	Test

Metric	l	SVM	S3VM	MR	Best Tuning	SVM	S3VM	MR	Best Tuning	
AUROC	10	0.63	0.64	0.72	0.61	0.63	0.64	0.67	0.61	Test
	100	0.87	0.87	0.87	0.87	0.87	0.86	0.87	0.86	Test

Table 4: Aggregate test results averaged over the 80 trials (8 datasets, 10 trials each) in a particular setting.

outperforms SVM in fewer trials than the other algorithms in some settings for these two metrics. This is because Best Tuning conservatively selects SVM in many trials. The take home message is that tuning using CV based on accuracy (and to a lesser extent maxF1) appears to mitigate some risk involved in applying SSL. AUROC, on the other hand, does not appear as effective for this purpose. Table 3 (bottom) shows that, for $u = 1000$, Best Tuning is worse than SVM fewer times, but for $u = 100$, MR achieves better performance overall.

We also compare overall average test performance (across datasets) for each metric and l,u combination. Table 4 reports these results for accuracy, maxF1, and AUROC. In terms of accuracy, we see that the Best Tuning approach leads to better performance than SVM, S3VM, or MR in all settings when averaged over datasets. We appear to achieve some synergy in dynamically choosing a different algorithm in each trial. In terms of maxF1, Best Tuning, S3VM, and MR are all at least as good as SL in three of the four l,u settings, and nearly as good in the fourth. Based on AUROC, though, the results are mixed depending on the specific setting. Notably, though, Best Tuning consistently leads to worse performance than SL when using this metric.

8.3 A Note on Cloud Computing

The experiments were carried out using the Condor High-Throughput Computing platform (Thain et al., 2005). We ran many trials per algorithm (using different datasets, l, u, and metrics). Each trial involved training hundreds of models using different parameter configurations repeated across five folds, and then training once more using the selected parameters. In the end, we trained a grand total of 794,880 individual models to produce the results in Table 2. Through distributed computing on approximately 50 machines in parallel, we were able to run all these experiments in less than a week, while using roughly three months worth of CPU time.

9 Conclusions

We have explored "realistic SSL," where all parameters are tuned via 5-fold cross validation, to simulate a real-world experience of trying to use unlabeled data in a novel NLP task. Our medium-scale empirical study of SVM, S3VM, and MR revealed that no algorithm is always superior, and furthermore that there are cases in which each SSL algorithm we examined can perform worse than SVM (in some cases significantly worse across 10 trials). To mitigate such risks, we proposed a simple meta-level procedure that selects one of the three models based on tuning performance. While cross validation is often dismissed for model selection in SSL due to a lack of labeled data, this Best Tuning approach proves effective in helping to ensure that incorporating unlabeled data does not hurt performance. Interestingly, this works well only when optimizing accuracy during tuning. For future work, we plan to extend this study to include additional datasets, algorithms, and tuning criteria. We also plan to develop more sophisticated techniques for choosing which SL/SSL algorithm to use in practice.

Acknowledgments

A. Goldberg is supported in part by a Yahoo! Key Technical Challenges Grant.

References

Mikhail Belkin, Partha Niyogi, and Vikas Sindhwani. 2006. Manifold regularization: A geometric framework for learning from labeled and unlabeled examples. *Journal of Machine Learning Research*, 7:2399–2434, November.

Avrim Blum and Tom Mitchell. 1998. Combining labeled and unlabeled data with co-training. In *COLT: Proceedings of the Workshop on Computational Learning Theory.*

Ulf Brefeld and Tobias Scheffer. 2006. Semi-supervised learning for structured output variables. In *ICML06, 23rd International Conference on Machine Learning*, Pittsburgh, USA.

R. Bruce and J. Wiebe. 1994. Word-sense disambiguation using decomposable models. In *Proceedings of the 32nd Annual Meeting of the Association for Computational Linguistics*, pages 139–146.

Lijuan Cai and Thomas Hofmann. 2003. Text categorization by boosting automatically extracted concepts. In *SIGIR '03: Proceedings of the 26th annual international ACM SIGIR conference on Research and development in informaion retrieval.*

Olivier Chapelle and Alexander Zien. 2005. Semi-supervised classification by low density separation. In *Proceedings of the Tenth International Workshop on Artificial Intelligence and Statistics (AISTAT 2005).*

Olivier Chapelle, Alexander Zien, and Bernhard Schölkopf, editors. 2006. *Semi-supervised learning.* MIT Press.

Tom Fawcett. 2004. ROC graphs: Notes and practical considerations for researchers. Technical Report HPL-2003-4.

Andrew B. Goldberg, Nathanael Fillmore, David Andrzejewski, Zhiting Xu, Bryan Gibson, and Xiaojin Zhu. 2009. May all your wishes come true: A study of wishes and how to recognize them. In *Proceedings of NAACL HLT.*

Thorsten Joachims. 1999. Making large-scale svm learning practical. In B. Schölkopf, C. Burges, and A. Smola, editors, *Advances in Kernel Methods - Support Vector Learning*. MIT Press.

M. Karlen, J. Weston, A. Erkan, and R. Collobert. 2008. Large scale manifold transduction. In Andrew McCallum and Sam Roweis, editors, *Proceedings of the 25th Annual International Conference on Machine Learning (ICML 2008)*, pages 448–455. Omnipress.

Vikas Sindhwani and S. Sathiya Keerthi. 2007. Newton methods for fast solution of semi-supervised linear SVMs. In Leon Bottou, Olivier Chapelle, Dennis DeCoste, and Jason Weston, editors, *Large-Scale Kernel Machines*. MIT Press.

V. Sindhwani and D. Rosenberg. 2008. An rkhs for multi-view learning and manifold co-regularization. In Andrew McCallum and Sam Roweis, editors, *Proceedings of the 25th Annual International Conference on Machine Learning (ICML 2008)*, pages 976–983. Omnipress.

Vikas Sindhwani, Partha Niyogi, and Mikhail Belkin. 2005. Beyond the point cloud: from transductive to semi-supervised learning. In *ICML05, 22nd International Conference on Machine Learning.*

Vikas Sindhwani, Sathiya Keerthi, and Olivier Chapelle. 2006. Deterministic annealing for semi-supervised kernel machines. In *ICML06, 23rd International Conference on Machine Learning*, Pittsburgh, USA.

Douglas Thain, Todd Tannenbaum, and Miron Livny. 2005. Distributed computing in practice: the condor experience. *Concurrency - Practice and Experience*, 17(2-4):323–356.

Xiaojin Zhu. 2005. Semi-supervised learning literature survey. Technical Report 1530, Department of Computer Sciences, University of Wisconsin, Madison.

Is Unlabeled Data Suitable for Multiclass SVM-based Web Page Classification?

Arkaitz Zubiaga, Víctor Fresno, Raquel Martínez
NLP & IR Group at UNED
Lenguajes y Sistemas Informáticos
E.T.S.I. Informática, UNED
{azubiaga, vfresno, raquel}@lsi.uned.es

Abstract

Support Vector Machines present an interesting and effective approach to solve automated classification tasks. Although it only handles binary and supervised problems by nature, it has been transformed into multiclass and semi-supervised approaches in several works. A previous study on supervised and semi-supervised SVM classification over binary taxonomies showed how the latter clearly outperforms the former, proving the suitability of unlabeled data for the learning phase in this kind of tasks. However, the suitability of unlabeled data for multiclass tasks using SVM has never been tested before. In this work, we present a study on whether unlabeled data could improve results for multiclass web page classification tasks using Support Vector Machines. As a conclusion, we encourage to rely only on labeled data, both for improving (or at least equaling) performance and for reducing the computational cost.

1 Introduction

The amount of web documents is increasing in a very fast way in the last years, what makes more and more complicated its organization. For this reason, web page classification has gained importance as a task to ease and improve information access. Web page classification can be defined as the task of labeling and organizing web documents within a set of predefined categories. In this work, we focus on web page classification based on Support Vector Machines (SVM, (Joachims, 1998)). This kind of classification tasks rely on a previously labeled training set of documents, with which the classifier acquires the required ability to classify new unknown documents.

Different settings can be distinguished for web page classification problems. On the one hand, attending to the learning technique the system bases on, it may be *supervised*, with all the training documents previously labeled, or *semi-supervised*, where unlabeled documents are also taken into account during the learning phase. On the other hand, attending to the number of classes, the classification may be *binary*, where only two possible categories can be assigned to each document, or *multiclass*, where three or more categories can be set. The former is commonly used for filtering systems, whereas the latter is necessary for bigger taxonomies, e.g. topical classification.

Although multiple studies have been made for text classification, its application to the web page classification area remains without enough attention (Qi and Davison, 2007). Analyzing the nature of a web page classification task, we can consider it to be, generally, multiclass problems, where it is usual to find numerous classes. In the same way, if we take into account that the number of available labeled documents is tiny compared to the size of the Web, this task becomes semi-supervised besides multiclass.

However, the original SVM algorithm supports neither semi-supervised learning nor multiclass taxonomies, due to its dichotomic and supervised nature. To solve this issue, different studies for both multiclass SVM and semi-supervised SVM approaches have been proposed, but a little effort has

Proceedings of the NAACL HLT Workshop on Semi-supervised Learning for Natural Language Processing, pages 28–36,
Boulder, Colorado, June 2009.

been invested in the combination of them.

(Joachims, 1999) compares supervised and semi-supervised approaches for binary tasks using SVM. It shows encouraging results for the transductive semi-supervised approach, clearly improving the supervised, and so he proved unlabeled data to be suitable to optimize binary SVM classifiers' results. On the other hand, the few works presented for semi-supervised multiclass SVM classification do not provide clear information on whether the unlabeled data improves the classification results in comparison with the only use of labeled data.

In this work, we performed an experiment among different SVM-based multiclass approaches, both supervised and semi-supervised. The experiments were focused on web page classification, and were carried out over three benchmark datasets: *BankSearch*, *WebKB* and *Yahoo! Science*. Using the results of the comparison, we analyze and study the suitability of unlabeled data for multiclass SVM classification tasks. We discuss these results and evaluate whether it is worthy to rely on a semi-supervised SVM approach to conduct this kind of tasks.

The remainder of this document is organized as follows. Next, in section 2, we briefly explain how SVM classifiers work for binary classifications, both for a supervised and a semi-supervised view. In section 3, we continue with the adaptation of SVM to multiclass environments, and show what has been done in the literature. Section 4 presents the details of the experiments carried out in this work, aim at evaluating the suitability of unlabeled data for multiclass SVM classification. In section 5 we show and discuss the results of the experiments. Finally, in section 6, we conclude with our thoughts and future work.

2 Binary SVM

In the last decade, SVM has become one of the most studied techniques for text classification, due to the positive results it has shown. This technique uses the vector space model for the documents' representation, and assumes that documents in the same class should fall into separable spaces of the representation. Upon this, it looks for a hyperplane that separates the classes; therefore, this hyperplane should maximize the distance between it and the nearest documents, what is called the margin. The following function is used to define the hyperplane (see Figure 1):

$$f(x) = w \cdot x + b$$

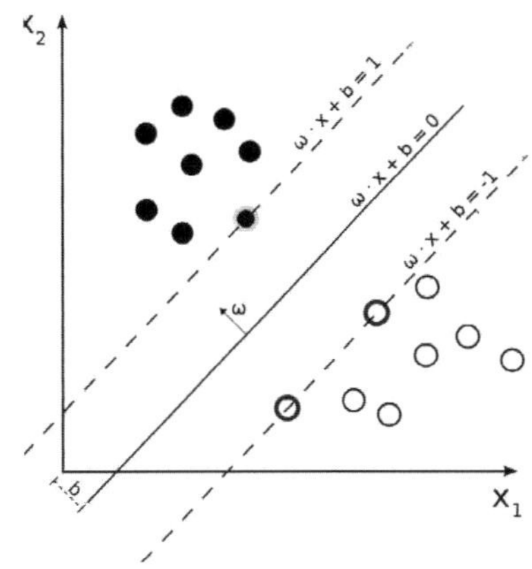

Figure 1: An example of binary SVM classification, separating two classes (black dots from white dots)

In order to resolve this function, all the possible values should be considered and, after that, the values of w and b that maximize the margin should be selected. This would be computationally expensive, so the following equivalent function is used to relax it (Boser et al. , 1992) (Cortes and Vapnik, 1995):

$$\min \left[\frac{1}{2}||w||^2 + C \sum_{i=1}^{l} \xi_i^d \right]$$

$$\text{Subject to:} \quad y_i(w \cdot x_i + b) \geq 1 - \xi_i, \xi_i \geq 0$$

where C is the penalty parameter, ξ_i is an stack variable for the ith document, and l is the number of labeled documents.

This function can only resolve linearly separable problems, thus the use of a kernel function is commonly required for the redimension of the space; in this manner, the new space will be linearly separable. After that, the redimension is undone, so the found hyperplane will be transformed to the original space, respecting the classification function. Best-known kernel functions include linear, polynomial, radial basis function (RBF) and sigmoid, among others. Different kernel functions' performance has been studied in (Schölkopf and Smola, 1999) and (Kivinen et al., 2002).

Note that the function above can only resolve binary and supervised problems, so different variants are necessary to perform semi-supervised or multiclass tasks.

2.1 Semi-supervised Learning for SVM (S^3VM)

Semi-supervised learning approaches differ in the learning phase. As opposed to supervised approaches, unlabeled data is used during the learning phase, and so classifier's predictions over them is also included as labeled data to learn. The fact of taking into account unlabeled data to learn can improve the classification done by supervised methods, specially when its predictions provide new useful information, as shown in figure 2. However, the noise added by erroneus predictions can make worse the learning phase and, therefore, its final performance. This makes interesting the study on whether relying on semi-supervised approaches is suitable for each kind of task.

Semi-supervised learning for SVM, also known as S^3VM, was first introduced by (Joachims, 1999) in a transductive way, by modifying the original SVM function. To do that, he proposed to add an additional term to the optimization function:

$$\min \left[\frac{1}{2} \cdot ||\omega||^2 + C \cdot \sum_{i=1}^{l} \xi_i^d + C^* \cdot \sum_{j=1}^{u} \xi_j^{*d} \right]$$

where *u* is the number of unlabeled data.

Nevertheless, the adaptation of SVM to semi-supervised learning significantly increases its computational cost, due to the non-convex nature of the resulting function, and so obtaining the minimum value is even more complicated. In order to relax the function, convex optimization techniques such as semi-definite programming are commonly used (Xu et al. , 2007), where minimizing the function gets much easier.

By means of this approach, (Joachims, 1999) demonstrated a large performance gap between the original supervised SVM and his semi-supervised proposal, in favour of the latter one. He showed that for binary classification tasks, the smaller is the training set size, the larger gets the difference among these two approaches. Although he worked with multiclass datasets, he splitted the problems into smaller binary ones, and so he did not demonstrate whether the same performance gap occurs for multiclass classification. This paper tries to cover this issue. (Chapelle et al., 2008) present a comprehensive study on S^3VM approaches.

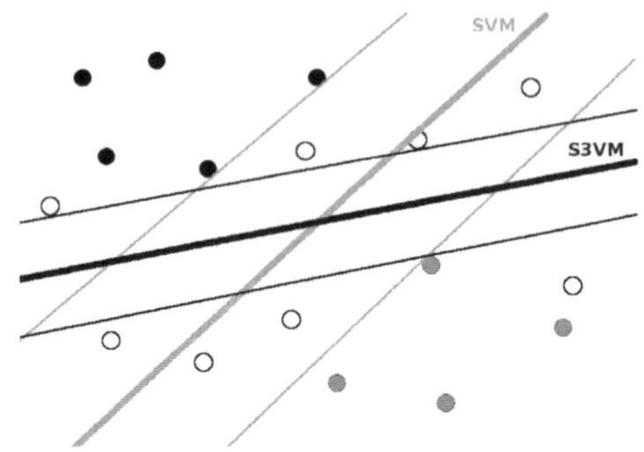

Figure 2: SVM vs S^3VM, where white balls are unlabeled documents

3 Multiclass SVM

Due to the dichotomic nature of SVM, it came up the need to implement new methods to solve multiclass problems, where more than two classes must be considered. Different approaches have been proposed to achieve this. On the one hand, as a direct approach, (Weston, 1999) proposed modifying the optimization function getting into account all the *k* classes at once:

$$\min \left[\frac{1}{2} \sum_{m=1}^{k} ||w_m||^2 + C \sum_{i=1}^{l} \sum_{m \neq y_i} \xi_i^m \right]$$

Subject to:

$$w_{y_i} \cdot x_i + b_{y_i} \geq w_m \cdot x_i + b_m + 2 - \xi_i^m, \xi_i^m \geq 0$$

On the other hand, the original binary SVM classifier has usually been combined to obtain a multiclass solution. As combinations of binary SVM classifiers, two different approaches to *k-class* classifiers can be emphasized (Hsu and Lin, 2002):

- *one-against-all* constructs *k* classifiers defining that many hyperplanes; each of them separates the class *i* from the rest *k-1*. For instance, for a problem with 4 classes, *1 vs 2-3-4*, *2 vs 1-3-4*, *3 vs 1-2-4* and *4 vs 1-2-3* classifiers would be created. New documents will be categorized in the class of the classifier that maximizes the margin: $\hat{C}_i = \arg\max_{i=1,\dots,k}(w_i x + b_i)$. As the number of classes increases, the amount of classifiers will increase linearly.

- *one-against-one* constructs $\frac{k(k-1)}{2}$ classifiers, one for each possible category pair. For instance, for a problem with 4 classes, *1 vs 2*, *1 vs 3*, *1 vs 4*, *2 vs 3*, *2 vs 4* and *3 vs 4* classifiers would be created. After that, it classifies each new document by using all the classifiers, where a vote is added for the winning class over each classifier; the method will propose the class with more votes as the result. As the number of classes increases, the amount of classifiers will increase in an exponential way, and so the problem could became very expensive for large taxonomies.

Both (Weston, 1999) and (Hsu and Lin, 2002) compare the direct multiclass approach to the *one-against-one* and *one-against-all* binary classifier combining approaches. They agree concluding that the direct approach does not outperform the results by *one-against-one* nor *one-against-all*, although it considerably reduces the computational cost because the number of support vector machines it constructs is lower. Among the binary combining approaches, they show the performance of *one-against-one* to be superior to *one-against-all*.

Although these approaches have been widely used in supervised learning environments, they have scarcely been applied to semi-supervised learning. Because of this, we believe the study on its applicability and performance for this type of problems could be interesting.

3.1 Multiclass S^{3}VM

When the taxonomy is defined by more than two classes and the number of previously labeled documents is very small, the combination of both multiclass and semi-supervised approaches could be required. That is, a multiclass S^{3}VM approach. The usual web page classification problem meets with these characteristics, since more than two classes are usually needed, and the tiny amount of labeled documents requires the use of unlabeled data for the learning phase.

Actually, there are a few works focused on transforming SVM into a semi-supervised and multiclass approach. As a direct approach, a proposal by (Yajima and Kuo, 2006) can be found. They modify the function for multiclass SVM classification and get it usable for semi-supervised tasks. The resulting optimization function is as follows:

$$\min \frac{1}{2}\sum_{i=1}^{h} \beta^{i^T} K^{-1} \beta^i$$

$$+C\sum_{j=1}^{l}\sum_{i \neq y_j} \max\{0, 1-(\beta_j^{y_j} - \beta_j^i)\}^2$$

where β represents the product of a vector of variables and a kernel matrix defined by the author.

On the other hand, some other works are based on different approaches to achieve a multiclass S^{3}VM classifier.

(Qi et al., 2004) use Fuzzy C-Means (FCM) to predict labels for unlabeled documents. After that, multiclass SVM is used to learn with the augmented training set, classifying the test set. (Xu y Schuurmans, 2005) rely on a clustering-based approach to label the unlabeled data. Afterwards, they apply a multiclass SVM classifier to the fully labeled training set. (Chapelle et al., 2006) present a direct multiclass S^{3}VM approach by using the Continuation Method. On the other hand, this is the only work, to the best of our knowledge, that has tested the *one-against-all* and *one-against-one* approaches in a semi-supervised environment. They apply these methods to some news datasets, for which they get low performance. Additionally, they show that *one-against-one* is not sufficient for real-world multiclass semi-supervised learning, since the unlabeled data cannot be restricted to the two classes under consideration.

It is noteworthy that most of the above works only presented their approaches and compared them to other semi-supervised classifying methods, such as Expectation-Maximization (EM) or Naive Bayes. As an exception, (Chapelle et al., 2006) compared a semi-supervised and a supervised SVM approach, but only over image datasets. Against this, we felt the need to evaluate and compare multiclass SVM and multiclass S^{3}VM approaches, for the sake of discovering whether learning with unlabeled web documents is helpful for multiclass problems when using SVM as a classifier.

4 Multiclass SVM versus Multiclass S^3VM

The main goal of this work is to evaluate the real contribution of unlabeled data for multiclass SVM-based web page classification tasks. There are a few works using semi-supervised multiclass SVM classifiers, but nobody has demonstrated it improves supervised SVM classifier's performance. Next, we detail the experiments we carried out to clear up any doubts and to ensure which is better for multiclass SVM-based web page classifications.

4.1 Approaches

In order to evaluate and compare multiclass SVM and multiclass S^3VM, we decided to use three different but equivalent approaches for each view, supervised and semi-supervised. For further information on these approaches, see section 3. We add a suffix, *-SVM* or *-S^3VM*, to the names of the approaches, to differentiate whether they are based in a supervised or a semi-supervised algorithm.

On the part of the semi-supervised view, the following three approaches were selected:

- *2-steps-SVM:* we called *2-steps-SVM* to the technique based on the direct multiclass supervised approach exposed in section 3. This method works, on its first step, with the training collection, learning with the labeled documents and predicting the unlabeled ones; after that, the latter documents are labeled based on the generated predictions. On the second step, now with a fully labeled training set, the usual supervised classification process is done, learning with the training documents and predicting the documents in the test set.

  This approach is somehow similar to those proposed by (Qi et al., 2004) and (Xu y Schurmans, 2005). Nonetheless, the *2-steps-SVM* approach uses the same method for both the first and second steps. A supervised multiclass SVM is used to increase the labeled set and, after that, to classify the test set.

- *one-against-all-S^3VM:* the *one-against-all* approach has not sufficiently been tested for semi-supervised environments, and seems interesting to evaluate its performance.

- *one-against-one-S^3VM:* the *one-against-one* does not seem to be suitable for semi-supervised environments, since the classifier is not able to ignore the inadecuate unlabeled documents for each 1-vs-1 binary task, as stated by (Chapelle et al., 2006). Anyway, since it has scarcely been tested, we also consider this approach.

On the other hand, the approaches selected for the supervised view were these: (1) *1-step-SVM*; (2) *one-against-all-SVM*, and (3) *one-against-one-SVM*.

The three approaches mentioned above are analogous to the semi-supervised approaches, *2-steps-SVM*, *one-against-all-S^3VM* and *one-against-one-S^3VM*, respectively. They differ in the learning phase: unlike the semi-supervised approaches, these three supervised approaches only rely on the labeled documents for the learning task, but after that they classify the same test documents. These approaches allow to evaluate whether the unlabeled documents are contributing in a positive or negative way in the learning phase.

4.2 Datasets

For these experiments we have used three web page benchmark datasets previously used for classification tasks:

- *BankSearch* (Sinka and Corne, 2002), a collection of 11,000 web pages over 11 classes, with very different topics: commercial banks, building societies, insurance agencies, java, c, visual basic, astronomy, biology, soccer, motorsports and sports. We removed the category sports, since it includes both soccer and motorsports in it, as a parent category. This results 10,000 web pages over 10 categories. 4,000 instances were assigned to the training set, while the other 6,000 were left on the test set.

- *WebKB*[1], with a total of 4,518 documents of 4 universities, and classified into 7 classes

[1] http://www.cs.cmu.edu/afs/cs.cmu.edu/project/theo-20/www/data/

(student, faculty, personal, department, course, project and other). The class named *other* was removed due to its ambiguity, and so we finally got 6 classes. 2,000 instances fell into the training set, and 2,518 to the test set.

- *Yahoo! Science* (Tan, 2002), with 788 scientific documents, classified into 6 classes (agriculture, biology, earth science, math, chemistry and others). We selected 200 documents for the training set, and 588 for the test set.

Within the training set, for each dataset, multiple versions were created, modifying the number of labeled documents, while the rest were left unlabeled. Thus, the size of labeled subset within the training set changes, ranging from 50 web documents to the whole training set.

4.3 Document Representation

SVM requires a vectorial representation of the documents as an input for the classifier, both for train and test phases. To obtain this vectorial representation, we first converted the original html files into plain text files, removing all the html tags. After that, we removed the noisy tokens, such as URLs, email addresses or some stopwords. For these edited documents, the *tf-idf* term weighting function was used to define the values for the uniterms found on the texts. As the term dimensionality became too large, we then removed the least-frequent terms by its document frequency; terms appearing in less than 0.5% of the documents were removed for the representation. The remaining uniterms define the vector space dimensions. That derived term vectors with 8285 dimensions for *BankSearch* dataset, 3115 for *WebKB* and 8437 for *Yahoo! Science*.

4.4 Implementation

To carry out our experiments, we based on freely available and already tested and experimented software. Different SVM classifiers were needed to implement the methods described in section 4.1.

SVMlight[2] was used to work with binary semi-supervised classifiers for the *one-against-all-S^3VM* and *one-against-one-S^3VM* approaches. In the same way, we implemented their supervised versions, *one-against-all-SVM* and *one-against-one-SVM*, in order to evaluate the contribution of unlabeled data. To achieve the supervised approaches, we ignored the unlabeled data during the training phase and, after that, tested with the same test set used for semi-supervised approaches. The default settings using a polynomial kernel were selected for the experiments.

SVMmulticlass[3] was used to implement the *2-steps-SVM* approach, by using it two times. Firstly, to train the labeled data and classify unlabeled data. After that, to train with the whole training set labeled with classifier's predictions, and to test with the test set. In the same way, the *1-step-SVM* method was implemented by ignoring unlabeled data and training only the labeled data. This method allows to evaluate the contribution of unlabeled data for the *2-steps-SVM* method.

4.5 Evaluation Measures

For the evaluation of the experiments we used the *accuracy* to measure the performance, since it has been frequently used for text classification problems, specially for multiclass tasks. The accuracy offers the percent of the correct predictions for the whole test set. We have considered the same weight for all the correct guesses for any class. A correct prediction in any of the classes has the same value, thus no weighting exists.

On the other hand, an averaged accuracy evaluation is also possible for the binary combining approaches. An averaged accuracy makes possible to evaluate the results by each binary classifier, and provides an averaged value for the whole binary classifier set. It is worth to note that these values do not provide any information for the evaluation of the combined multiclass results, but only for evaluating each binary classifier before combining them.

5 Results and Discussion

Next, we show and discuss the results of our experiments. It is remarkable that both *one-against-one-SVM* and *one-against-one-S^3VM* approaches were very inferior to the rest, and so we decided not to plot them in order to maintain graphs' clarity. Hence, figures 3, 4 and 5 show the results in accordance

[2] http://svmlight.joachims.org

[3] http://www.cs.cornell.edu/People/tj/svm_light/svm_multiclass.html

with the labeled subset size for the *2-steps-SVM*, *1-step-SVM*, *one-against-all-S*^{3}*VM* and *one-against-all-SVM* approaches within our experiments. For the results to be more representative, nine executions were done for each subset, obtaining the mean value. These nine executions vary on the labeled subset within the training set.

The fact that *one-against-one-S*^{3}*VM* has been the worst approach for our experiments confirms that the noise added by the unlabeled documents within each 1-vs-1 binary classification task is harmful to the learning phase, and it is not corrected when merging all the binary tasks.

The averaged accuracy for the combined binary classifiers allows to compare the *one-against-one* and *one-against-all* views. The averaged accuracy for *one-against-one-S*^{3}*VM* shows very low performance (about 60% in most cases), whereas the same value for *one-against-all-S*^{3}*VM* is much higher (about 90% in most cases). This is obvious to happen for the *one-against-all* view, since it is much easier to predict documents not pertaining to the class under consideration for each *1-vs-all* binary classifier. Although each binary classifier gets about 90% accuracy for the *one-against-one-S*^{3}*VM* approach, this value falls considerably when combining them to get the multiclass result. This shows the additional difficulty for multiclass problems compared to binary ones. Hence, the difficulty to correctly predict unlabeled data increases for multiclass tasks, and it is more likely to add noise during the learning phase.

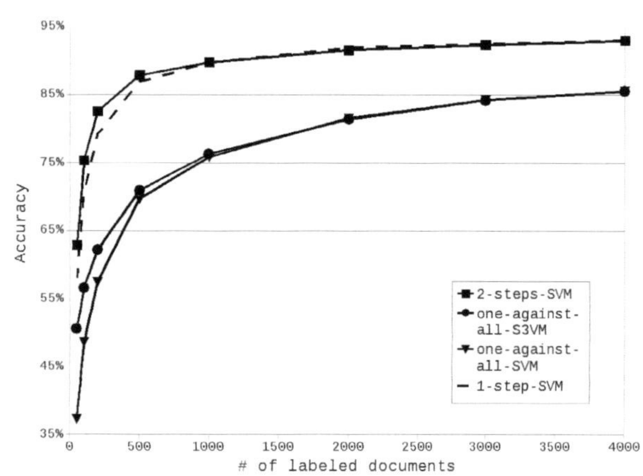

Figure 3: Results for BankSearch dataset

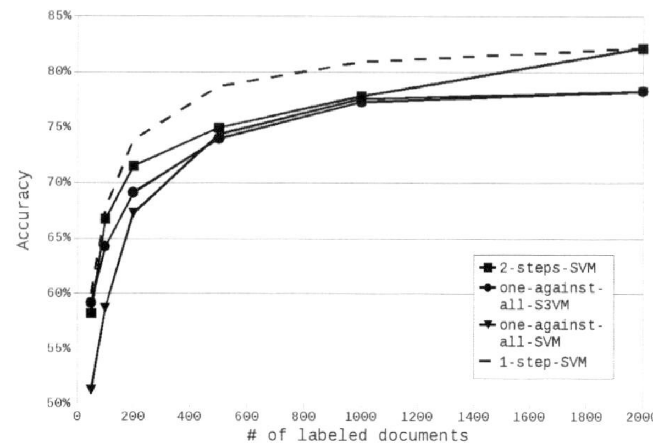

Figure 4: Results for WebKB dataset

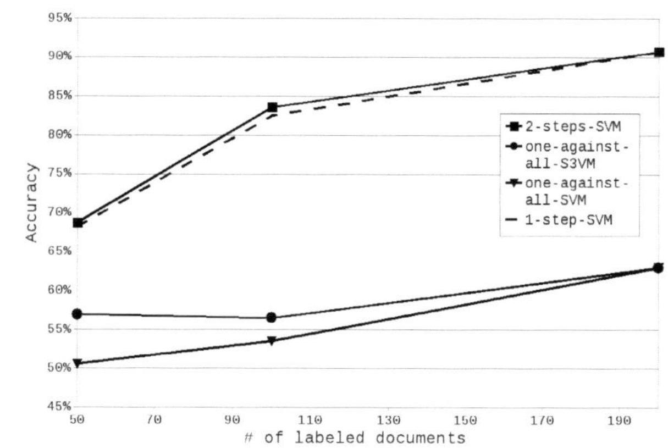

Figure 5: Results for Yahoo! Science dataset

For all the datasets we worked with, there is a noticeable performance gap between direct multiclass and binary combining approaches. Both *2-steps-SVM* and *1-step-SVM* are always on the top of the graphs, and *one-against-all-S*^{3}*VM* and *one-against-all-SVM* approaches are so far from catching up with their results, except for *WebKB* dataset, where the gap is not so noticeable. This seems encouraging, since considering less support vectors in a direct multiclass approach reduces the computational cost and improves the final results.

Comparing the two analogous approaches among them, different conclusions could be extracted. On the one hand, *one-against-all-S*^{3}*VM* shows slightly better results than *one-against-all-SVM*, and so considering unlabeled documents seems to be favourable for the *one-against-all* view. On the other hand, the direct multiclass view shows varying results. Both *2-steps-SVM* and *1-step-SVM* show very similar results for *BankSearch* and *Yahoo! Science* datasets, but superior for *1-step-SVM* over the *WebKB* dataset. As a conclusion of this, ignoring unlabeled documents by means of the *1-step-SVM* approach seems to be advisable, since it reduces the computation cost, obtaining at least the same results than the semi-supervised *2-steps-SVM*.

Although their results are so poor, as we said above, the supervised approach wins for the *one-against-one* view; this confirms, again, that the *one-against-one* view is not an adecuate view to be applied in a semi-supervised environment, due to the noise existing during the learning phase.

When analyzing the performance gaps between the analogous approaches, a general conclusion can be extracted: the smaller is the labeled subset the bigger is the performance gap, except for the *Yahoo! Science* dataset. Comparing the two best approaches, *1-step-SVM* and *2-steps-SVM*, the performance gap increases when the number of labeled documents decrease for *BankSearch*; for this dataset, the accuracy by *1-step-SVM* is 0.92 times the one by *2-steps-SVM* when the number of labeled documents is only 50, but this proportion goes to 0.99 with 500 labeled documents. This reflects how the contribution of unlabeled data decreases while the labeled set increases. For *WebKB*, the performance gap is in favour of *1-step-SVM*, and varies between 1.01 and 1.05 times *2-steps-SVM* method's accuracy, even with only 50 labeled documents. Again, increasing the labeled set negatively affects semi-supervised algorithm's performance. Last, for *Yahoo! Science*, the performance gap among these two approaches is not considerable, since their results are very similar.

Our conjecture for the performance difference between *1-step-SVM* and *2-steps-SVM* for the three datasets is the nature of the classes. The accuracy by semi-supervised *2-steps-SVM* is slightly higher for *BankSearch* and *Yahoo! Science*, where the classes are quite heterogeneous. On the other hand, the accuracy by supervised *1-step-SVM* is clearly higher for *WebKB*, where all the classes are an academic topic, and so more homogeneous. The semi-supervised classifiers show a major problem for predicting the unlabeled documents when the collection is more homogeneous, and so more difficult to differ between classes.

In summary, the main idea is that unlabeled documents do not seem to contribute as they would for multiclass tasks using SVM. Within the approaches we tested, the supervised *1-step-SVM* approach shows the best (or very similar to the best in some cases) results in accuracy and, taking into account it is the least-expensive approach, we strongly encourage to use this approach to solve multiclass web page classification tasks, mainly when the classes under consideration are homogeneous.

6 Conclusions and Outlook

We have studied and analyzed the contribution of considering unlabeled data during the learning phase for multiclass web page classification tasks using SVM. Our results show that ignoring unlabeled document to learn reduces computational cost and, additionaly, obtains similar or slightly worse accuracy values for heterogeneus taxonomies, but higher for homogeneous ones. Therefore we show that, unlike for binary cases, as was shown by (Joachims, 1999), a supervised view outperforms a semi-supervised one for multiclass environments. Our thought is that predicting unlabeled documents' class is much more difficult when the number of classes increases, and so, the mistaken labeled documents are harmful for classifier's learning phase.

As a future work, a direct semi-supervised multiclass approach, such as those proposed by (Yajima and Kuo, 2006) and (Chapelle et al., 2006), should also be considered, as well as setting the classifier with different parameters or kernels. Balancing the weight of previously and newly labeled data could also be interesting to improve semi-supervised approaches' results.

Acknowledgments

We wish to thank the anonymous reviewers for their helpful and instructive comments. This work has been supported by the Research Network MAVIR (S-0505/TIC-0267), the Regional Ministry of Education of the Community of Madrid, and by the Spanish Ministry of Science and Innovation project QEAVis-Catiex (TIN2007-67581-C02-01).

References

B. E. Boser, I. Guyon and V. Vapnik. 1992. A Training Algorithm for Optimal Margin Classifiers. *Proceedings of the 5th Annual Workshop on computational Learning Theory*.

C. Campbell. 2000. Algorithmic Approaches to Training Support Vector Machines: A Survey *Proceedings of ESANN'2000, European Symposium on Artificial Neural Networks*.

O. Chapelle, M. Chi y A. Zien 2006. A Continuation Method for Semi-supervised SVMs. *Proceedings of ICML'06, the 23rd International Conference on Machine Learning*.

O. Chapelle, V. Sindhwani, S. Keerthi 2008. Optimization Techniques for Semi-Supervised Support Vector Machines. *J. Mach. Learn. Res.*.

C. Cortes and V. Vapnik. 1995. Support Vector Network. *Machine Learning*.

C.-H. Hsu and C.-J. Lin. 2002. A Comparison of Methods for Multiclass Support Vector Machines. *IEEE Transactions on Neural Networks*.

T. Joachims. 1998. Text Categorization with Support Vector Machines: Learning with many Relevant Features. *Proceedings of ECML98, 10th European Conference on Machine Learning*.

T. Joachims. 1999. Transductive Inference for Text Classification Using Support Vector Machines. *Proceedings of ICML99, 16th International Conference on Machine Learning*.

J. Kivinen and E.J. Smola and R.C. Williamson. 2002. Learning with Kernels.

T. Mitchell. 1997. *Machine Learning*. McGraw Hill.

H.-N. Qi, J.-G. Yang, Y.-W. Zhong y C. Deng 2004. Multi-class SVM Based Remote Sensing Image Classification and its Semi-supervised Improvement Scheme. *Proceedings of the 3rd ICMLC*.

X. Qi and B.D. Davison. 2007. Web Page Classification: Features and Algorithms. *Technical Report LU-CSE-07-010*.

B. Schölkopf and A. Smola. 1999. *Advances in Kernel Methods: Support Vector Learning*. MIT Press.

F. Sebastiani. 2002. Machine Learning in Automated Text Categorization. *ACM Computing Surveys, pp. 1-47*.

M.P. Sinka and D.W. Corne. 2002. A New Benchmark Dataset for Web Document Clustering. *Soft Computing Systems*.

C.M. Tan, Y.F. Wang and C.D. Lee. 2002. The Use of Bigrams to Enhance Text Categorization. *Information Processing and Management*.

J. Weston and C. Watkins. 1999. Multi-class Support Vector Machines. *Proceedings of ESAAN, the European Symposium on Artificial Neural Networks*.

L. Xu y D. Schuurmans. 2005. Unsupervised and Semi-supervised Multiclass Support Vector Machines. *Proceedings of AAAI'05, the 20th National Conference on Artificial Intelligence*.

Z. Xu, R. Jin, J. Zhu, I. King and M. R. Lyu. 2007. Efficient Convex Optimization for Transductive Support Vector Machine. *Advances in Neural Information Processing Systems*.

Y. Yajima and T.-F. Kuo. 2006. Optimization Approaches for Semi-Supervised Multiclass Classification. *Proceedings of ICDM'06 Workshops, the 6th International Conference on Data Mining*.

A Comparison of Structural Correspondence Learning and Self-training for Discriminative Parse Selection

Barbara Plank
University of Groningen, The Netherlands
b.plank@rug.nl

Abstract

This paper evaluates two semi-supervised techniques for the adaptation of a parse selection model to Wikipedia domains. The techniques examined are *Structural Correspondence Learning* (SCL) (Blitzer et al., 2006) and *Self-training* (Abney, 2007; McClosky et al., 2006). A preliminary evaluation favors the use of SCL over the simpler self-training techniques.

1 Introduction and Motivation

Parse selection constitutes an important part of many parsing systems (Hara et al., 2005; van Noord and Malouf, 2005; McClosky et al., 2006). Yet, there is little to no work focusing on the *adaptation* of parse selection models to novel domains. This is most probably due to the fact that potential gains for this task are inherently bounded by the underlying grammar. The few studies on adapting parse disambiguation models, like Hara et al. (2005), have focused exclusively on *supervised domain adaptation*, i.e. one has access to a comparably small, but labeled amount of target data. In contrast, in *semi-supervised domain adaptation* one has only *unlabeled* target data. It is a more realistic situation, but at the same time also considerably more difficult.

In this paper we evaluate two semi-supervised approaches to domain adaptation of a discriminative parse selection model. We examine *Structural Correspondence Learning* (SCL) (Blitzer et al., 2006) for this task, and compare it to several variants of *Self-training* (Abney, 2007; McClosky et al., 2006). For empirical evaluation (section 4) we use the Alpino parsing system for Dutch (van Noord and Malouf, 2005). As target domain, we exploit Wikipedia as primary test and training collection.

2 Previous Work

So far, Structural Correspondence Learning has been applied successfully to PoS tagging and Sentiment Analysis (Blitzer et al., 2006; Blitzer et al., 2007). An attempt was made in the CoNLL 2007 shared task to apply SCL to non-projective dependency parsing (Shimizu and Nakagawa, 2007). However, the system just ended up at rank 7 out of 8 teams. Based on annotation differences in the datasets (Dredze et al., 2007) and a bug in their system (Shimizu and Nakagawa, 2007), their results are inconclusive. A recent attempt (Plank, 2009) shows promising results on applying SCL to parse disambiguation. In this paper, we extend that line of work and compare SCL to bootstrapping approaches such as self-training.

Studies on self-training have focused mainly on generative, constituent based parsing (Steedman et al., 2003; McClosky et al., 2006; Reichart and Rappoport, 2007). Steedman et al. (2003) as well as Reichart and Rappoport (2007) examine self-training for PCFG parsing in the small seed case ($< 1k$ labeled data), with different results. In contrast, McClosky et al. (2006) focus on large seeds and exploit a reranking-parser. Improvements are obtained (McClosky et al., 2006; McClosky and Charniak, 2008), showing that a reranker is necessary for successful self-training in such a high-resource scenario. While they self-trained a generative model, we examine self-training and SCL for semi-supervised adaptation of a discriminative parse selection system.

Proceedings of the NAACL HLT Workshop on Semi-supervised Learning for Natural Language Processing, pages 37–42,
Boulder, Colorado, June 2009.

3 Semi-supervised Domain Adaptation

3.1 Structural Correspondence Learning

Structural Correspondence Learning (Blitzer et al., 2006) exploits unlabeled data from both source and target domain to find correspondences among features from different domains. These correspondences are then integrated as new features in the labeled data of the source domain. The outline of SCL is given in Algorithm 1.

The key to SCL is to exploit *pivot features* to automatically identify feature correspondences. Pivots are features occurring frequently and behaving similarly in both domains (Blitzer et al., 2006). They correspond to auxiliary problems in Ando and Zhang (2005). For every such pivot feature, a binary classifier is trained (step 2 of Algorithm 1) by masking the pivot feature in the data and trying to predict it with the remaining non-pivot features. Non-pivots that correlate with many of the same pivots are assumed to correspond. These pivot predictor weight vectors thus implicitly align non-pivot features from source and target domain. Intuitively, if we are able to find good correspondences through 'linking' pivots, then the augmented source data should transfer better to a target domain (Blitzer et al., 2006).

Algorithm 1 SCL (Blitzer et al., 2006)

1: Select m pivot features.
2: Train m binary classifiers (pivot predictors). Create matrix $W_{n \times m}$ of binary predictor weight vectors $W = [w_1, .., w_m]$, with n number of nonpivots.
3: Dimensionality Reduction. Apply SVD to W: $W_{n \times m} = U_{n \times n} D_{n \times m} V^T_{m \times m}$ and select $\theta = U^T_{[1:h,:]}$ (the h top left singular vectors of W).
4: Train a new model on the original and new features obtained by applying the projection $x \cdot \theta$.

SCL for Discriminative Parse Selection So far, pivot features on the word level were used (Blitzer et al., 2006; Blitzer et al., 2007). However, for parse disambiguation based on a conditional model they are irrelevant. Hence, we follow Plank (2009) and actually first parse the unlabeled data. This allows a possibly noisy, but more abstract representation of the underlying data. Features thus correspond to properties of parses: application of grammar rules (*r1,r2* features), dependency relations (*dep*), PoS tags (*f1,f2*), syntactic features (*s1*), precedence (*mf*), bilexical preferences (*z*), apposition (*appos*) and further features for unknown words, temporal phrases, coordination (*h,in_year* and *p1*, respectively). These features are further described in van Noord and Malouf (2005).

Selection of pivot features As pivot features should be common across domains, here we restrict our pivots to be of the type *r1,p1,s1* (the most frequently occurring feature types). In more detail, *r1* indicates which grammar rule applied, *p1* whether coordination conjuncts are parallel, and *s1* whether local/non-local extraction occurred. We count how often each feature appears in the parsed source and target domain data, and select those *r1,p1,s1* features as *pivot features*, whose count is $> t$, where t is a specified threshold. In all our experiments, we set $t = 5000$. In this way we obtained on average 360 pivot features, on the datasets described in Section 4.

3.2 Self-training

Self-training (Algorithm 2) is a simple single-view bootstrapping algorithm. In self-training, the newly labeled instances are taken at face value and added to the training data.

There are many possible ways to instantiate self-training (Abney, 2007). One variant, introduced in Abney (2007) is the notion of '(in)delibility': in the *delible* case the classifier relabels all of the unlabeled data from scratch in every iteration. The classifier may become unconfident about previously selected instances and they may drop out (Steven Abney, personal communication). In contrast, in the *indelible* case, labels once assigned do not change again (Abney, 2007).

In this paper we look at the following variants of self-training:

- single versus multiple iterations,
- selection versus no selection (taking all self-labeled data or selecting presumably higher quality instances); different scoring functions for selection,
- delibility versus indelibility for multiple iterations.

Algorithm 2 Self-training (indelible) (Abney, 2007).

1: L_0 is labeled [seed] data, U is unlabeled data
2: $c \leftarrow train(L_0)$
3: **repeat**
4: $\quad L \leftarrow L + select(label(U - L, c))$
5: $\quad c \leftarrow train(L)$
6: **until** stopping criterion is met

Scoring methods We examine three simple scoring functions for instance selection: i) *Entropy* ($-\sum_{y \in Y(s)} p(\omega|s,\theta) \log p(\omega|s,\theta)$). ii) *Number of parses* ($|Y(s)|$); and iii) *Sentence Length* ($|s|$).

4 Experiments and Results

Experimental Design The system used in this study is Alpino, a two-stage dependency parser for Dutch (van Noord and Malouf, 2005). The first stage consists of a HPSG-like grammar that constitutes the parse generation component. The second stage is a Maximum Entropy (MaxEnt) parse selection model. To train the MaxEnt model, parameters are estimated based on informative samples (Osborne, 2000). A parse is added to the training data with a score indicating its "goodness" (van Noord and Malouf, 2005). The score is obtained by comparing it with the gold standard (if available; otherwise the score is approximated through parse probability).

The source domain is the Alpino Treebank (van Noord and Malouf, 2005) (newspaper text; approx. 7,000 sentences; 145k tokens). We use Wikipedia both as testset and as unlabeled target data source. We assume that in order to parse data from a very specific domain, say about the artist Prince, then data related to that domain, like information about the New Power Generation, the Purple rain movie, or other American singers and artists, should be of help. Thus, we exploit Wikipedia's category system to gather domain-specific target data. In our empirical setup, we follow Blitzer et al. (2006) and balance the size of source and target data. Thus, depending on the size of the resulting target domain dataset, and the "broadness" of the categories involved in creating it, we might wish to filter out certain pages. We implemented a filter mechanism that excludes pages of a certain category (e.g. a supercategory that is hypothesized to be "too broad"). Further details about the dataset construction are given in (Plank, 2009). Table 1 provides information on the target domain datasets constructed from Wikipedia.

Related to	Articles	Sents	Tokens	Relationship
Prince	290	9,772	145,504	filtered super
Paus	445	8,832	134,451	all
DeMorgan	394	8,466	132,948	all

Table 1: Size of related unlabeled data; relationship indicates whether all related pages are used or some are filtered out.

The size of the target domain testsets is given in Table 2. As evaluation measure concept accuracy (CA) (van Noord and Malouf, 2005) is used (similar to labeled dependency accuracy).

The training data for the pivot predictors are the 1-best parses of source and target domain data as selected by the original Alpino model. We report on results of SCL with dimensionality parameter set to $h = 25$, and remaining settings identical to Plank (2009) (i.e., no feature-specific regularization and no feature normalization and rescaling).

Baseline Table 2 shows the baseline accuracies (model trained on labeled out-of-domain data) on the Wikipedia testsets (last column: size in number of sentences). The second and third column indicate lower (first parse) and upper- (oracle) bounds.

Wikipedia article	baseline	first	oracle	sent
Prince (musician)	85.03	71.95	88.70	357
Paus Johannes Paulus II	85.72	74.30	89.09	232
Augustus De Morgan	80.09	70.08	83.52	254

Table 2: Supervised Baseline results.

SCL and Self-training results The results for SCL (Table 3) show a small, but consistent increase in absolute performance on all testsets over the baselines (up to $+0.27$ absolute CA or 7.34% relative error reduction, which is significant at $p < 0.05$ according to sign test).

In contrast, basic self-training (Table 3) achieves roughly only baseline accuracy and lower performance than SCL, with one exception. On the DeMorgan testset, self-training scores slightly higher than SCL. However, the improvements of both SCL and self-training are not significant on this rather small testset. Indeed, self-training scores better than the baseline on only 5 parses out of 254, while its performance is lower on 2, leaving only 3 parses that account for the difference.

	CA	ϕ	Rel.ER
Prince baseline	85.03	78.06	0.00
SCL	$\star$ 85.30	79.67	7.34
Self-train (all-at-once)	85.08	78.38	1.46
Paus baseline	85.72	77.23	0.00
SCL	85.82	77.87	2.81
Self-train (all-at-once)	85.78	77.62	1.71
DeMorgan baseline	80.09	74.44	0.00
SCL	80.15	74.92	1.88
Self-train (all-at-once)	80.24	75.63	4.65

Table 3: Results of SCL and self-training (single iteration, no selection). Entries marked with $\star$ are statistically significant at $p < 0.05$. The ϕ score incorporates upper- and lower-bounds.

To gauge whether other instantiations of self-training are more effective, we evaluated the self-training variants introduced in section 3.2 on the Prince dataset. In the iterative setting, we follow Steedman et al. (2003) and parse 30 sentences from which 20 are selected in every iteration.

With regard to the comparison of delible versus indelible self-training (whether labels may change), our empirical findings shows that the two cases achieve *very* similar performance; the two curves highly overlap (Figure 1). The accuracies of both curves fluctuate around 85.13, showing no upward or downward trend. In general, however, indelibility is preferred since it takes considerably less time (the classifier does not have to relabel U from scratch in every iteration). In addition, we tested EM (which uses all unlabeled data in each iteration). Its performance is consistently lower, varying around the baseline.

Figure 2 compares several self-training variants with the supervised baseline and SCL. It summarizes the effect of i) selection versus no selection (and various selection techniques) as well as ii) single versus multiple iterations of self-training. For clarity, the figure shows the learning curve of the best selection technique only, but depicts the performance of the various selection techniques in a single iteration (non-solid lines).

In the iterative setting, taking the whole self-labeled data and not selecting certain instances (grey curve in Figure 2) degrades performance. In contrast, selecting shorter sentences slightly improves accuracy, and is the best selection method among the ones tested (shorter sentences, entropy, fewer parses).

For all self-training instantiations, running multiple iterations is on average just the same as running a single iteration (the non-solid lines are roughly the average of the learning curves). Thus there is no real need to run several iterations of self-training.

The main conclusion is that in contrast to SCL, none of the self-training instantiations achieves a significant improvement over the baseline.

5 Conclusions and Future Work

The paper compares Structural Correspondence Learning (Blitzer et al., 2006) with (various instances of) self-training (Abney, 2007; McClosky et al., 2006) for the adaptation of a parse selection model to Wikipedia domains.

The empirical findings show that none of the evaluated self-training variants (delible/indelible, single versus multiple iterations, various selection techniques) achieves a significant improvement over the baseline. The more 'indirect' exploitation of unlabeled data through SCL is more fruitful than pure self-training. Thus, favoring the use of the more complex method, although the findings are not confirmed on all testsets.

Of course, our results are preliminary and, rather than warranting yet many definite conclusions, encourage further investigation of SCL (varying size of target data, pivots selection, bigger testsets as well as other domains etc.) as well as related semi-supervised adaptation techniques.

Acknowledgments

Thanks to Gertjan van Noord and the anonymous reviewers for their comments. The Linux cluster of the High-Performance Computing Center of the University of Groningen was used in this work.

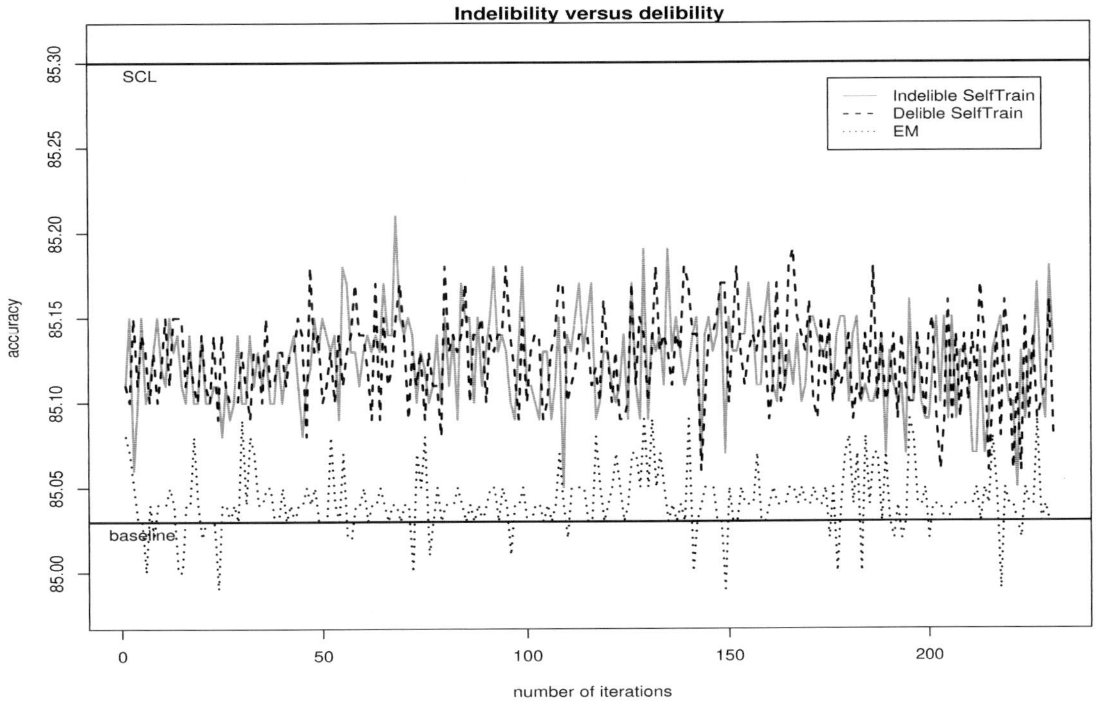

Figure 1: Delible versus Indelible self-training and EM. Delible and indelible self-training achieve *very* similar performance. However, indelibility is preferred over delibility since it is considerably faster.

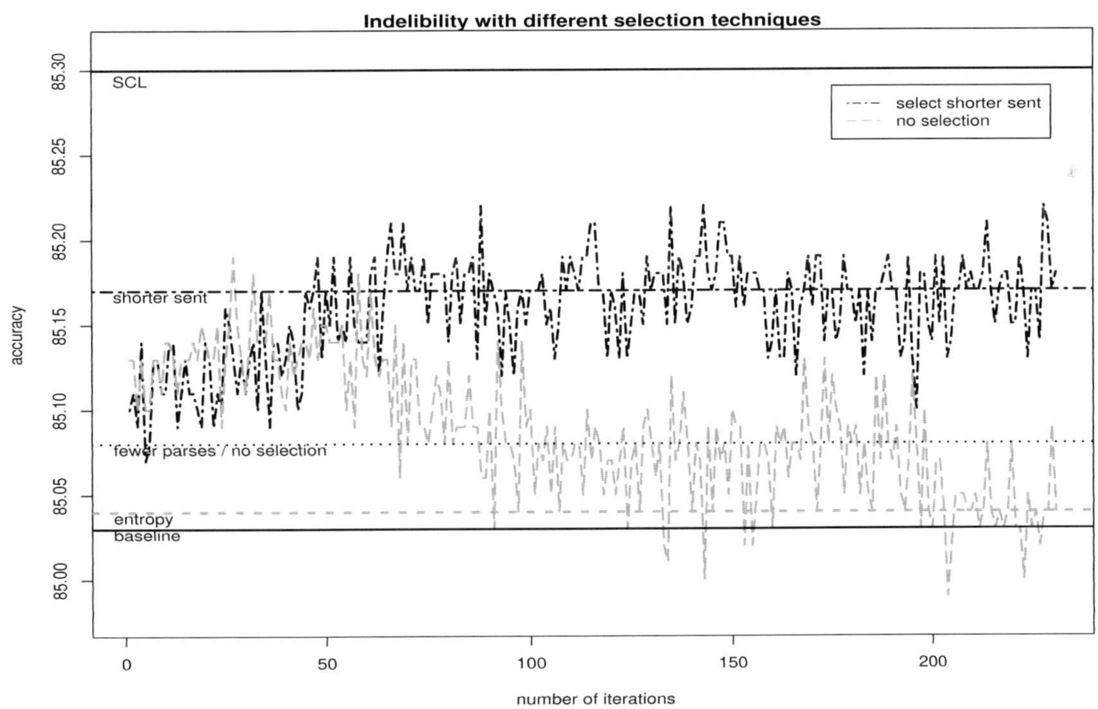

Figure 2: Self-training variants compared to supervised baseline and SCL. The effect of various selection techniques (Sec. 3.2) in a single iteration is depicted (non-solid lines; fewer parses and no selection achieve identical results). For clarity, the figure shows the learning curve for the best selection technique only (shorter sent) versus no selection. On average running multiple iterations is just the same as a single iteration. In all cases SCL still performs best.

References

Steven Abney. 2007. *Semi-supervised Learning for Computational Linguistics*. Chapman & Hall.

Rie Kubota Ando and Tong Zhang. 2005. A framework for learning predictive structures from multiple tasks and unlabeled data. *Journal of Machine Learning Research*, 6:1817–1853.

John Blitzer, Ryan McDonald, and Fernando Pereira. 2006. Domain adaptation with structural correspondence learning. In *Conference on Empirical Methods in Natural Language Processing*, Sydney, Australia.

John Blitzer, Mark Dredze, and Fernando Pereira. 2007. Biographies, bollywood, boom-boxes and blenders: Domain adaptation for sentiment classification. In *Association for Computational Linguistics*, Prague, Czech Republic.

Mark Dredze, John Blitzer, Pratha Pratim Talukdar, Kuzman Ganchev, Joao Graca, and Fernando Pereira. 2007. Frustratingly hard domain adaptation for parsing. In *Proceedings of the CoNLL Shared Task Session - Conference on Natural Language Learning*, Prague, Czech Republic.

Tadayoshi Hara, Miyao Yusuke, and Jun'ichi Tsujii. 2005. Adapting a probabilistic disambiguation model of an hpsg parser to a new domain. In *Proceedings of the International Joint Conference on Natural Language Processing*.

David McClosky and Eugene Charniak. 2008. Self-training for biomedical parsing. In *Proceedings of ACL-08: HLT, Short Papers*, pages 101–104, Columbus, Ohio, June. Association for Computational Linguistics.

David McClosky, Eugene Charniak, and Mark Johnson. 2006. Effective self-training for parsing. In *Proceedings of the Human Language Technology Conference of the NAACL, Main Conference*, pages 152–159, New York City. Association for Computational Linguistics.

Miles Osborne. 2000. Estimation of stochastic attribute-value grammars using an informative sample. In *Proceedings of the Eighteenth International Conference on Computational Linguistics (COLING 2000)*.

Barbara Plank. 2009. Structural correspondence learning for parse disambiguation. In *Proceedings of the Student Research Workshop at EACL 2009*, Athens, Greece, April.

Roi Reichart and Ari Rappoport. 2007. Self-training for enhancement and domain adaptation of statistical parsers trained on small datasets. In *Proceedings of Association for Computational Linguistics*, Prague.

Nobuyuki Shimizu and Hiroshi Nakagawa. 2007. Structural correspondence learning for dependency parsing. In *Proceedings of the CoNLL Shared Task Session of EMNLP-CoNLL 2007*.

Mark Steedman, Miles Osborne, Anoop Sarkar, Stephen Clark, Rebecca Hwa, Julia Hockenmaier, Paul Ruhlen, Steven Baker, and Jeremiah Crim. 2003. Bootstrapping statistical parsers from small datasets. In *In Proceedings of the EACL*, pages 331–338.

Gertjan van Noord and Robert Malouf. 2005. Wide coverage parsing with stochastic attribute value grammars. Draft. A preliminary version of this paper was published in the Proceedings of the IJCNLP workshop Beyond Shallow Analyses, Hainan China, 2004.

Latent Dirichlet Allocation with Topic-in-Set Knowledge*

David Andrzejewski
Computer Sciences Department
University of Wisconsin-Madison
Madison, WI 53706, USA
andrzeje@cs.wisc.edu

Xiaojin Zhu
Computer Sciences Department
University of Wisconsin-Madison
Madison, WI 53706, USA
jerryzhu@cs.wisc.edu

Abstract

Latent Dirichlet Allocation is an unsupervised graphical model which can discover latent topics in unlabeled data. We propose a mechanism for adding partial supervision, called topic-in-set knowledge, to latent topic modeling. This type of supervision can be used to encourage the recovery of topics which are more relevant to user modeling goals than the topics which would be recovered otherwise. Preliminary experiments on text datasets are presented to demonstrate the potential effectiveness of this method.

1 Introduction

Latent topic models such as Latent Dirichlet Allocation (LDA) (Blei et al., 2003) have emerged as a useful family of graphical models with many interesting applications in natural language processing. One of the key virtues of LDA is its status as a fully generative probabilistic model, allowing principled extensions and variations capable of expressing rich problem domain structure (Newman et al., 2007; Rosen-Zvi et al., 2004; Boyd-Graber et al., 2007; Griffiths et al., 2005).

LDA is an unsupervised learning model. This work aims to add supervised information in the form of latent topic assignments to LDA. Traditionally, topic assignments have been denoted by the variable z in LDA, and we will call such supervised information "z-labels." In particular, a z-label is the knowledge that the topic assignment for a given word position is within a subset of topics. As such, this work is a combination of unsupervised model and supervised knowledge, and falls into the category similar to constrained clustering (Basu et al., 2008) and semi-supervised dimensionality reduction (Yang et al., 2006).

1.1 Related Work

A similar but simpler type of topic labeling information has been applied to computer vision tasks. Topic modeling approaches have been applied to scene modeling (Sudderth et al., 2005), segmentation, and classification or detection (Wang and Grimson, 2008). In some of these vision applications, the latent topics themselves are assumed to correspond to object labels. If labeled data is available, either all (Wang and Mori, 2009) or some (Cao and Fei-Fei, 2007) of the z values can be treated as observed, rather than latent, variables. Our model extends z-labels from single values to subsets, thus offer additional model expressiveness.

If the topic-based representations of documents are to be used for document clustering or classification, providing z-labels for words can be seen as similar to semi-supervised learning with labeled features (Druck et al., 2008). Here the words are features, and z-label guidance acts as a feature label. This differs from other supervised LDA variants (Blei and McAuliffe, 2008; Lacoste-Julien et al., 2008) which use document label information.

The ΔLDA model for statistical software debugging (Andrzejewski et al., 2007) partitions the topics into 2 sets: "usage" topics which can appear in all

* We would like to acknowledge the assistance of Brandi Gancarz with the biological annotations. This work is supported in part by the Wisconsin Alumni Research Foundation.

Proceedings of the NAACL HLT Workshop on Semi-supervised Learning for Natural Language Processing, pages 43–48,
Boulder, Colorado, June 2009.

documents, and "bug" topics which can only appear in a special subset of documents. This effect was achieved by using different α hyperparameters for the 2 subsets of documents. z-labels can achieve the same effect by restricting the z's in documents outside the special subset, so that the z's cannot assume the "bug" topic values. Therefore, the present approach can be viewed as a generalization of ΔLDA.

Another perspective is that our z-labels may guide the topic model towards the discovery of secondary or non-dominant statistical patterns in the data (Chechik and Tishby, 2002). These topics may be more interesting or relevant to the goals of the user, but standard LDA would ignore them in favor of more prominent (and perhaps orthogonal) structure.

2 Our Model

2.1 Review of Latent Dirichlet Allocation

We briefly review LDA, following the notation of (Griffiths and Steyvers, 2004) [1]. Let there be T topics. Let $\mathbf{w} = w_1 \ldots w_n$ represent a corpus of D documents, with a total of n words. We use d_i to denote the document of word w_i, and z_i the hidden topic from which w_i is generated. Let $\phi_j^{(w)} = p(w|z = j)$, and $\theta_j^{(d)} = p(z = j)$ for document d. LDA involves the following generative model:

$$\begin{aligned} \theta &\sim \text{Dirichlet}(\alpha) && (1)\\ z_i|\theta^{(d_i)} &\sim \text{Multinomial}(\theta^{(d_i)}) && (2)\\ \phi &\sim \text{Dirichlet}(\beta) && (3)\\ w_i|z_i,\phi &\sim \text{Multinomial}(\phi_{z_i}), && (4) \end{aligned}$$

where α and β are hyperparameters for the document-topic and topic-word Dirichlet distributions, respectively. Even though they can be vector valued, for simplicity we assume α and β are scalars, resulting in symmetric Dirichlet priors.

Given our observed words $\mathbf{w}$, the key task is inference of the hidden topics $\mathbf{z}$. Unfortunately, this posterior is intractable and we resort to a Markov Chain Monte Carlo (MCMC) sampling scheme, specifically Collapsed Gibbs Sampling (Griffiths and Steyvers, 2004). The full conditional equation used for sampling individual z_i values from the posterior is given by

$$P(z_i = v|\mathbf{z}_{-i}, \mathbf{w}, \alpha, \beta) \propto \left(\frac{n_{-i,v}^{(d)} + \alpha}{\sum_u^T (n_{-i,u}^{(d)} + \alpha)}\right)\left(\frac{n_{-i,v}^{(w_i)} + \beta}{\sum_{w'}^W (\beta + n_{-i,v}^{(w')})}\right) \quad (5)$$

where $n_{-i,v}^{(d)}$ is the number of times topic v is used in document d, and $n_{-i,v}^{(w_i)}$ is the number of times word w_i is generated by topic v. The $-i$ notation signifies that the counts are taken omitting the value of z_i.

2.2 Topic-in-Set Knowledge: z-labels

Let

$$q_{iv} = \left(\frac{n_{-i,v}^{(d)} + \alpha}{\sum_u^T (n_{-i,u}^{(d)} + \alpha)}\right)\left(\frac{n_{-i,v}^{(w_i)} + \beta}{\sum_{w'}^W (\beta + n_{-i,v}^{(w')})}\right).$$

We now define our z-labels. Let $C^{(i)}$ be the set of possible z-labels for latent topic z_i. We set a hard constraint by modifying the Gibbs sampling equation with an indicator function $\delta(v \in C^{(i)})$, which takes on value 1 if $v \in C^{(i)}$ and is 0 otherwise:

$$P(z_i = v|\mathbf{z}_{-i}, \mathbf{w}, \alpha, \beta) \propto q_{iv}\delta(v \in C^{(i)}) \quad (6)$$

If we wish to restrict z_i to a single value (e.g., $z_i = 5$), this can now be accomplished by setting $C^{(i)} = \{5\}$. Likewise, we can restrict z_i to a subset of values $\{1, 2, 3\}$ by setting $C^{(i)} = \{1, 2, 3\}$. Finally, for unconstrained z_i we simply set $C^{(i)} = \{1, 2, ..., T\}$, in which case our modified sampling (6) reduces to the standard Gibbs sampling (5).

This formulation gives us a flexible method for inserting prior domain knowledge into the inference of latent topics. We can set $C^{(i)}$ independently for every single word w_i in the corpus. This allows us, for example, to force two occurrences of the same word (e.g., "Apple pie" and "Apple iPod") to be explained by different topics. This effect would be impossible to achieve by using topic-specific asymmetric β vectors and setting some entries to zero.

This hard constraint model can be relaxed. Let $0 \le \eta \le 1$ be the strength of our constraint, where $\eta = 1$ recovers the hard constraint (6) and $\eta = 0$ recovers unconstrained sampling (5):

$$P(z_i = v|\mathbf{z}_{-i}, \mathbf{w}, \alpha, \beta) \propto q_{iv}\left(\eta\delta(v \in C^{(i)}) + 1 - \eta\right).$$

[1] We enclose superscripts in parentheses in this paper.

While we present the z-label constraints as a mechanical modification to the Gibbs sampling equations, it can be derived from an undirected extension of LDA (omitted here) which encodes z-labels. The soft constraint Gibbs sampling equation arises naturally from this formulation, which is the basis for the First-Order Logic constraints described later in the future work section.

3 Experiments

We now present preliminary experimental results to demonstrate some interesting applications for topic-in-set knowledge. Unless otherwise specified, symmetric hyperparameters $\alpha = .5$ and $\beta = .1$ were used and all MCMC chains were run for 2000 samples before estimating ϕ and θ from the final sample, as in (Griffiths and Steyvers, 2004).

3.1 Concept Expansion

We explore the use of topic-in-set for identifying words related to a target concept, given a set of seed words associated with that concept. For example, a biological expert may be interested in the concept "translation". The expert would then provide a set of seed words which are strongly related to this concept, here we assume the seed word set {translation,trna,anticodon,ribosome}. We add the hard constraint that $z_i = 0$ for all occurrences of these four words in our corpus of approximately 9,000 yeast-related abstracts.

We ran LDA with the number of topics $T = 100$, both with and without the z-label knowledge on the seed words. Table 1 shows the most probable words in selected topics from both runs. Table 1a shows Topic 0 from the constrained run, while Table 1b shows the topics which contained seed words among the top 50 most probable words from the unconstrained run.

In order to better understand the results, these top words were annotated for relevance to the target concept (translation) by an outside biological expert. The words in Table 1 were then colored blue if they were one of the original seed words, red if they were judged as relevant, and left black otherwise. From a quick glance, we can see that Topic 0 from the constrained run contains more relevant terms than Topic 43 from the standard LDA run. Topic 31 has a similar number of relevant terms, but taken together we can see that the emphasis of Topic 31 is slightly off-target, more focused on "mRNA turnover" than "translation". Likewise, Topic 73 seems more focused on the ribosome itself than the process of translation. Overall, these results demonstrate the potential effectiveness of z-label information for guiding topic models towards a user-seeded concept.

3.2 Concept Exploration

Suppose that a user has chosen a set of terms and wishes to discover different topics related to these terms. By constraining these terms to only appear in a restricted set of topics, these terms will be *concentrated* in the set of topics. The split within those set of topics may be different from what a standard LDA will produce, thus revealing new information within the data.

To make this concrete, say we are interested in the location "United Kingdom". We seed this concept with the following LOCATION-tagged terms {britain, british, england, uk, u.k., wales, scotland, london}. These terms are then restricted to appear only in the first 3 topics. Our corpus is an entity-tagged Reuters newswire corpus used for the CoNLL-2003 shared task (Tjong Kim Sang and De Meulder, 2003). In order to focus on our target location, we also restrict all other LOCATION-tagged tokens to *not* appear in the first 3 topics. For this experiment we set $T = 12$, arrived at by trial-and-error in the baseline (standard LDA) case.

The 50 most probable words for each topic are shown in Figure 2, and tagged entities are prefixed with their tags for easy identification. Table 2a shows the top words for the first 3 topics of our z-label run. These three topics are all related to the target LOCATION United Kingdom, but they also split nicely into business, cricket, and soccer. Words which are highly relevant to each of these 3 concepts are colored blue, red, and green, respectively.

In contrast, in Table 2b we show topics from standard LDA which contain any of the "United Kingdom" LOCATION terms (which are underlined) among the 50 most probable words for that topic. We make several observations about these topics. First, standard LDA Topic 0 is mostly concerned with political unrest in Russia, which is not particu-

Topic 0	translation, ribosomal, trna, rrna, initiation, ribosome, protein, ribosomes, is, factor, processing, translational nucleolar, pre-rrna, synthesis, small, 60s, eukaryotic, biogenesis, subunit, trnas, subunits, large, nucleolus factors, 40, synthetase, free, modification, rna, depletion, eif-2, initiator, 40s, ef-3, anticodon, maturation 18s, eif2, mature, eif4e, associated, synthetases, aminoacylation, snornas, assembly, eif4g, elongation

(a) Topic 0 with z-label

Topic 31	mrna, translation, initiation, mrnas, rna, transcripts, 3, transcript, polya, factor, 5, translational, decay, codon decapping, factors, degradation, end, termination, eukaryotic, polyadenylation, cap, required, efficiency synthesis, show, codons, abundance, rnas, aug, nmd, messenger, turnover, rna-binding, processing, eif2, eif4e eif4g, cf, occurs, pab1p, cleavage, eif5, cerevisiae, major, primary, rapid, tail, efficient, upf1p, eif-2
Topic 43	type, is, wild, yeast, trna, synthetase, both, methionine, synthetases, class, trnas, enzyme, whereas, cytoplasmic because, direct, efficiency, presence, modification, aminoacylation, anticodon, either, eukaryotic, between different, specific, discussed, results, similar, some, met, compared, aminoacyl-trna, able, initiator, sam not, free, however, recognition, several, arc1p, fully, same, forms, leads, identical, responsible, found, only, well
Topic 73	ribosomal, rrna, protein, is, processing, ribosome, ribosomes, rna, nucleolar, pre-rrna, rnase, small, biogenesis depletion, subunits, 60s, subunit, large, synthesis, maturation, nucleolus, associated, essential, assembly components, translation, involved, rnas, found, component, mature, rp, 40s, accumulation, 18s, 40, particles snornas, factors, precursor, during, primary, rrnas, 35s, has, 21s, specifically, results, ribonucleoprotein, early

(b) Standard LDA Topics

Figure 1: Concept seed words are colored blue, other words judged relevant to the target concept are colored red.

larly related to the target location. Second, Topic 2 is similar to our previous business topic, but with a more US-oriented slant. Note that "dollar" appears with high probability in standard LDA Topic 2, but not in our z-label LDA Topic 0. Standard LDA Topic 8 appears to be a mix of both soccer and cricket words. Therefore, it seems that our topic-in-set knowledge helps in distilling topics related to the seed words.

Given this promising result, we attempted to repeat this experiment with some other nations (United States, Germany, China), but without much success. When we tried to restrict these LOCATION words to the first few topics, these topics tended to be used to explain other concepts unrelated to the target location (often other sports). We are investigating the possible causes of this problem.

4 Conclusions and Future Work

We have defined Topic-in-Set knowledge and demonstrated its use within LDA. As shown in the experiments, the partial supervision provided by z-labels can encourage LDA to recover topics relevant to user interests. This approach combines the pattern-discovery power of LDA with user-provided guidance, which we believe will be very attractive to practical users of topic modeling.

Future work will deal with at least two important issues. First, when will this form of partial supervision be most effective or appropriate? Our experimental results suggest that this approach will struggle if the user's target concepts are simply not prevalent in the text. Second, can we modify this approach to express richer forms of partial supervision? More sophisticated forms of knowledge may allow users to specify their preferences or prior knowledge more effectively. Towards this end, we are investigating the use of First-Order Logic in specifying prior knowledge. Note that the set z-labels presented here can be expressed as simple logical formulas. Extending our model to general logical formulas would allow the expression of more powerful relational preferences.

References

David Andrzejewski, Anne Mulhern, Ben Liblit, and Xiaojin Zhu. 2007. Statistical debugging using latent topic models. In Stan Matwin and Dunja Mladenic, editors, *18th European Conference on Machine Learning*, Warsaw, Poland.

Topic 0	million, company, 's, year, shares, net, profit, half, group, [I-ORG]corp, market, sales, share, percent expected, business, loss, stock, results, forecast, companies, deal, earnings, statement, price, [I-LOC]london billion, [I-ORG]newsroom, industry, newsroom, pay, pct, analysts, issue, services, analyst, profits, sale added, firm, [I-ORG]london, chief, quarter, investors, contract, note, tax, financial, months, costs
Topic 1	[I-LOC]england, [I-LOC]london, [I-LOC]britain, cricket, [I-PER]m., overs, test, wickets, scores, [I-PER]ahmed [I-PER]paul, [I-PER]wasim, innings, [I-PER]a., [I-PER]akram, [I-PER]mushtaq, day, one-day, [I-PER]mark, final [I-LOC]scotland, [I-PER]waqar, [I-MISC]series, [I-PER]croft, [I-PER]david, [I-PER]younis, match, [I-PER]ian total, [I-MISC]english, [I-PER]khan, [I-PER]mullally, bat, declared, fall, [I-PER]d., [I-PER]g., [I-PER]j. bowling, [I-PER]r., [I-PER]robert, [I-PER]s., [I-PER]steve, [I-PER]c. captain, golf, tour, [I-PER]sohail, extras [I-ORG]surrey
Topic 2	soccer, division, results, played, standings, league, matches, halftime, goals, attendance, points, won, [I-ORG]st drawn, saturday, [I-MISC]english, lost, premier, [I-MISC]french, result, scorers, [I-MISC]dutch, [I-ORG]united [I-MISC]scottish, sunday, match, [I-LOC]london, [I-ORG]psv, tabulate, [I-ORG]hapoel, [I-ORG]sydney, friday summary, [I-ORG]ajax, [I-ORG]manchester, tabulated, [I-MISC]german, [I-ORG]munich, [I-ORG]city [I-MISC]european, [I-ORG]rangers, summaries, weekend, [I-ORG]fc, [I-ORG]sheffield, wednesday, [I-ORG]borussia [I-ORG]fortuna, [I-ORG]paris, tuesday

(a) Topics with set z-labels

Topic 0	police, 's, people, killed, [I-MISC]russian, friday, spokesman, [I-LOC]moscow, told, rebels, group, officials [I-PER]yeltsin, arrested, found, miles, km, [I-PER]lebed, capital, thursday, tuesday, [I-LOC]chechnya, news saturday, town, authorities, airport, man, government, state, agency, plane, reported, security, forces city, monday, air, quoted, students, region, area, local, [I-LOC]russia, [I-ORG]reuters, military, [I-LOC]london held, southern, died
Topic 2	percent, 's, market, thursday, july, tonnes, week, year, lower, [I-LOC]u.s., rate, prices, billion, cents, dollar friday, trade, bank, closed, trading, higher, close, oil, bond, fell, markets, index, points, rose demand, june, rates, september, traders, [I-ORG]newsroom, day, bonds, million, price, shares, budget, government growth, interest, monday, [I-LOC]london, economic, august, expected, rise
Topic 5	's, match, team, win, play, season, [I-MISC]french, lead, home, year, players, [I-MISC]cup, back, minutes champion, victory, time, n't, game, saturday, title, side, set, made, wednesday, [I-LOC]england league, run, club, top, good, final, scored, coach, shot, world, left, [I-MISC]american, captain [I-MISC]world, goal, start, won, champions, round, winner, end, years, defeat, lost
Topic 8	division, [I-LOC]england, soccer, results, [I-LOC]london, [I-LOC]pakistan, [I-MISC]english, matches, played standings, league, points, [I-ORG]st, cricket, saturday, [I-PER]ahmed, won, [I-ORG]united, goals [I-PER]wasim, [I-PER]akram, [I-PER]m., [I-MISC]scottish, [I-PER]mushtaq, drawn, innings, premier, lost [I-PER]waqar, test, [I-PER]croft, [I-PER]a., [I-PER]younis, declared, wickets, [I-ORG]hapoel, [I-PER]mullally [I-ORG]sydney, day, [I-ORG]manchester, [I-PER]khan, final, scores, [I-PER]d., [I-MISC]german, [I-ORG]munich [I-PER]sohail, friday, total, [I-LOC]oval
Topic 10	[I-LOC]germany, 's, [I-LOC]italy, [I-LOC]u.s., metres, seconds, [I-LOC]france, [I-LOC]britain, [I-LOC]russia world, race, leading, [I-LOC]sweden, [I-LOC]australia, [I-LOC]spain, women, [I-MISC]world, [I-LOC]belgium [I-LOC]netherlands, [I-PER]paul, [I-LOC]japan, [I-MISC]olympic, [I-LOC]austria, [I-LOC]kenya, men, time results, [I-LOC]brussels, [I-MISC]cup, [I-LOC]canada, final, minutes, record, [I-PER]michael, meeting, round [I-LOC]norway, friday, scores, [I-PER]mark, [I-PER]van, [I-LOC]ireland, [I-PER]peter, [I-MISC]grand [I-MISC]prix, points, saturday, [I-LOC]finland, cycling, [I-ORG]honda

(b) Standard LDA Topics

Figure 2: Topics containing "United Kingdom" location words. Words related to business are colored blue, cricket red, and soccer green.

Sugato Basu, Ian Davidson, and Kiri Wagstaff, editors. 2008. *Constrained Clustering: Advances in Algorithms, Theory, and Applications*. Chapman & Hall/CRC Press.

David Blei and Jon McAuliffe. 2008. Supervised topic models. In J.C. Platt, D. Koller, Y. Singer, and S. Roweis, editors, *Advances in Neural Information Processing Systems 20*, pages 121–128. MIT Press,

Cambridge, MA.

David M. Blei, Andrew Y. Ng, and Michael I. Jordan. 2003. Latent Dirichlet allocation. *Journal of Machine Learning Research*, 3:993–1022.

Jordan Boyd-Graber, David Blei, and Xiaojin Zhu. 2007. A topic model for word sense disambiguation. In *Proceedings of the 2007 Joint Conference on Empirical Methods in Natural Language Processing and Computational Natural Language Learning (EMNLP-CoNLL)*, pages 1024–1033.

Liangliang Cao and Li Fei-Fei. 2007. Spatially coherent latent topic model for concurrent segmentation and classification of objects and scenes. In *ICCV*, pages 1–8.

Gal Chechik and Naftali Tishby. 2002. Extracting relevant structures with side information. In *NIPS 15*, pages 857–864. MIT press.

Gregory Druck, Gideon Mann, and Andrew McCallum. 2008. Learning from labeled features using generalized expectation criteria. In *SIGIR 2008*, pages 595–602, New York, NY, USA. ACM.

Thomas Griffiths and Mark Steyvers. 2004. Finding scientific topics. *Proceedings of the National Academy of Sciences*, 101(suppl. 1):5228–5235.

Thomas L. Griffiths, Mark Steyvers, David M. Blei, and Joshua B. Tenenbaum. 2005. Integrating topics and syntax. In *NIPS 17*.

S. Lacoste-Julien, F. Sha, and M. Jordan. 2008. Disclda: Discriminative learning for dimensionality reduction and classification. In *Advances in Neural Information Processing Systems 21 (NIPS08)*.

David Newman, Kat Hagedorn, Chaitanya Chemudugunta, and Padhraic Smyth. 2007. Subject metadata enrichment using statistical topic models. In *JCDL '07: Proceedings of the 7th ACM/IEEE-CS joint conference on Digital libraries*, pages 366–375, New York, NY, USA. ACM.

Michal Rosen-Zvi, Thomas Griffiths, Mark Steyvers, and Padhraic Smyth. 2004. The author-topic model for authors and documents. In *Proceedings of the 20th conference on Uncertainty in artificial intelligence (UAI)*, pages 487–494, Arlington, Virginia, United States. AUAI Press.

Erik B. Sudderth, Antonio B. Torralba, William T. Freeman, and Alan S. Willsky. 2005. Learning hierarchical models of scenes, objects, and parts. In *ICCV*, pages 1331–1338.

Erik Tjong Kim Sang and Fien De Meulder. 2003. Introduction to the conll-2003 shared task: Language-independent named entity recognition. In *Proceedings of CoNLL-2003*, pages 142–147, Edmonton, Canada.

Xiaogang Wang and Eric Grimson. 2008. Spatial latent dirichlet allocation. In J.C. Platt, D. Koller, Y. Singer, and S. Roweis, editors, *NIPS 20*, pages 1577–1584. MIT Press, Cambridge, MA.

Yang Wang and Greg Mori. 2009. Human action recognition by semi-latent topic models. In *IEEE Transactions on Pattern Analysis and Machine Intelligence*.

Xin Yang, Haoying Fu, Hongyuan Zha, and Jesse Barlow. 2006. Semi-supervised nonlinear dimensionality reduction. In *ICML-06, 23nd International Conference on Machine Learning*.

An Analysis of Bootstrapping for the Recognition of Temporal Expressions

Jordi Poveda
TALP Research Center
Technical University of Catalonia (UPC)
Barcelona, Spain
jpoveda@lsi.upc.edu

Mihai Surdeanu
NLP Group
Stanford University
Stanford, CA
mihais@stanford.edu

Jordi Turmo
TALP Research Center
Technical University of Catalonia (UPC)
Barcelona, Spain
turmo@lsi.upc.edu

Abstract

We present a semi-supervised (bootstrapping) approach to the extraction of time expression mentions in large unlabelled corpora. Because the only supervision is in the form of seed examples, it becomes necessary to resort to heuristics to rank and filter out spurious patterns and candidate time expressions. The application of bootstrapping to time expression recognition is, to the best of our knowledge, novel. In this paper, we describe one such architecture for bootstrapping Information Extraction (IE) patterns —suited to the extraction of entities, as opposed to events or relations— and summarize our experimental findings. These point out to the fact that a pattern set with a good increase in recall with respect to the seeds is achievable within our framework while, on the other side, the decrease in precision in successive iterations is succesfully controlled through the use of ranking and selection heuristics. Experiments are still underway to achieve the best use of these heuristics and other parameters of the bootstrapping algorithm.

1 Introduction

The problem of time expression recognition refers to the identification in free-format natural language text of the occurrences of expressions that denote time. Time-denoting expressions appear in a great diversity of forms, beyond the most obvious absolute time or date references (e.g. *11pm*, *February 14th, 2005*): time references that anchor on another time (*three hours after midnight*, *two weeks before Christmas*), expressions denoting durations (*a few months*), expressions denoting recurring times (*every third month*, *twice in the hour*), context-dependent times (*today*, *last year*), vague references (*somewhere in the middle of June*, *the near future*) or times that are indicated by an event (*the day G. Bush was reelected*). This problem is a subpart of a task called TERN (Temporal Expression Recognition and Normalization), where temporal expressions are first identified in text and then its intended temporal meaning is represented in a canonical format. TERN was first proposed as an independent task in the 2004 edition of the ACE conferences[1]. The most widely used standard for the annotation of temporal expressions is TIMEX (Ferro et al., 2005).

The most common approach to temporal expression recognition in the past has been the use of hand-made grammars to capture the expressions (see (Wiebe et al., 1998; Filatova and Hovy, 2001; Saquete et al., 2004) for examples), which can then be easily expanded with additional attributes for the normalization task, based on computing distance and direction (past or future) with respect to a reference time. This approach achieves an F_1-measure of approximately 85% for recognition and normalization. The use of machine learning techniques — mainly statistical— for this task is a more recent development, either alongside the traditional hand-grammar approach to learn to distinguish specific difficult cases (Mani and Wilson, 2000), or on its own (Hacioglu et al., 2005). The latter apply SVMs to the recognition task alone, using the output of several human-made taggers as additional features for the classifier, and report an F_1-measure of 87.8%.

[1] http://www.nist.gov/speech/tests/ace/

Proceedings of the NAACL HLT Workshop on Semi-supervised Learning for Natural Language Processing, pages 49–57,
Boulder, Colorado, June 2009.

Bootstrapping techniques have been used for such diverse NLP problems as: word sense disambiguation (Yarowsky, 1995), named entity classification (Collins and Singer, 1999), IE pattern acquisition (Riloff, 1996; Yangarber et al., 2000; Yangarber, 2003; Stevenson and Greenwood, 2005), document classification (Surdeanu et al., 2006), fact extraction from the web (Paşca et al., 2006) and hyponymy relation extraction (Kozareva et al., 2008).

(Yarowsky, 1995) used bootstrapping to train decision list classifiers to disambiguate between two senses of a word, achieving impressive classification accuracy. (Collins and Singer, 1999) applied bootstrapping to extract rules for named entity (NE) classification, seeding the sytem with a few handcrafted rules. Their main innovation was to split training in two alternate stages: during one step, only contextual rules are sought; during the second step, the new contextual rules are used to tag further NEs and these are used to produce new spelling rules.

Bootstrapping approaches are employed in (Riloff, 1996), (Yangarber et al., 2000), (Yangarber, 2003), and (Stevenson and Greenwood, 2005) in order to find IE patterns for domain-specific event extraction. (Paşca et al., 2006) employ a bootstrapping process to extract general facts from the Web, viewed as two-term relationships (e.g [Donald Knuth, 1938] could be an instance of a "born in year" relationship). (Surdeanu et al., 2006) used bootstrapping co-trained with an EM classifier in order to perform topic classification of documents based on the presence of certain learned syntactic-semantic patterns. In (Kozareva et al., 2008), bootstrapping is applied to finding new members of certain class of objects (i.e. an "is-a" relationship), by providing a member of the required class as seed and using a "such as" type of textual pattern to locate new instances.

The recognition of temporal expressions is crucial for many applications in NLP, among them: IE, Question Answering (QA) and Automatic Summarization (for the temporal ordering of events). Work on slightly supervised approaches such as bootstrapping is justified by the large availability of unlabelled corpora, as opposed to tagged ones, from which to learn models for recognition.

2 Architecture

Figure 1 illustrates the building blocks of the algorithm and their interactions, along with input and output data.

The inputs to the bootstrapping algorithm are the unlabelled training corpus and a file of seed examples. The unlabelled corpus is a large collection of documents which has been tokenized, POS tagged, lemmatized, and syntactically analyzed for basic syntactic constituents (shallow parsing) and headwords. The second input is a set of *seed examples*, consisting of a series of token sequences which we assume to be correct time expressions. The seeds are supplied without additional features, and without context information.

Our bootstrapping algorithm works with two alternative views of the same target data (time expressions), that is: *patterns* and *examples* (i.e. an instance of a pattern in the corpus). A *pattern* is a generalized representation that can match any sequence of tokens meeting the conditions expressed in the pattern (these can be morphological, semantic, syntactic and contextual). An *example* is an actual candidate occurrence of a time expression. Patterns are generated from examples found in the corpus and, in its turn, new examples are found by searching for matches of new patterns. Both patterns and examples may carry contextual information, that is, a window of tokens left and right of the candidate time expression.

Output examples and *output patterns* are the outputs of the bootstrapping process. Both the set of *output examples* and the set of *output patterns* are increased with each new iteration, by adding the new candidate examples (respectively, patterns) that have been "accepted" during the last iteration (i.e. those that have passed the ranking and selection step).

Initially, a single pass through the corpus is performed in order to find occurrences of the seeds in the text. Thus, we bootstrap an initial set of *examples*. From then on, the bootstrapping process consists of a succession of iterations with the following steps:

1. Ranking and selection of examples: Each example produced during any of the previous iterations, 0 to $i - 1$, is assigned a score (ranking). The top n examples are selected to grow the set of output examples (selection) and will

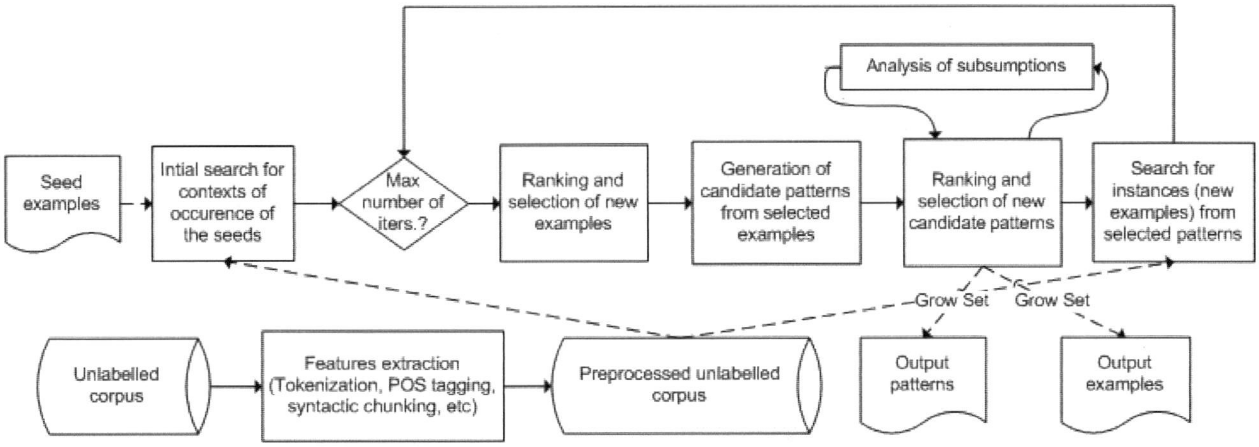

Figure 1: Block diagram of bootstrapping algorithm

be used for the next step. The details are given in Section 4.2.

2. Generation of candidate patterns: Candidate patterns for the current iteration are generated from the selected examples of the previous step (discussed in Section 3).
3. Ranking and selection of candidate patterns: Each pattern from the current iteration is assigned a score and the top m patterns are selected to grow the set of output patterns and to be used in the next step (discussed in Section 4.1). This step also involves a process of analysis of subsumptions, performed simultaneously with selection, in which the set of selected patterns is examined and those that are subsumed by other patterns are discarded.
4. Search for instances of the selected patterns: The training corpus is traversed, in order to search for instances (matches) of the selected patterns, which, together with the accepted examples from all previous iterations, will form the set of candidate examples for iteration $i+1$.

Also, in order to relax the matching of patterns to corpus tokens and of token forms among themselves, the matching of token forms is case-insensitive, and all the digits in a token are generalized to a generic digit marker (for instance, "12-23-2006" is internally rewritten as "@@-@@-@@@@").

Even though our architecture is built on a traditional boostrapping approach, there are several elements that are novel, at least in the context of temporal expression recognition: a) our pattern representation incorporates full syntax and distributional semantics in a unified model (see Section 3); b) our pattern ranking/selection approach includes a subsumption model to limit redundancy; c) the formulae in our example ranking/selection approach are designed to work with variable-length expressions that incorporate a context.

3 Pattern representation

Patterns capture both the sequence of tokens that integrate a potential time expression (i.e. a time expression mention), and information from the left and right context where it occurs (up to a bounded length). Let us call *prefix* the part of the pattern that represents the left context, *infix* the part that represents a potential time expression mention and *postfix* the part that represents the right context.

The EBNF grammar that encodes our pattern representation is given in Figure 2. Patterns are composed of multiple *pattern elements* (PEs). A pattern element is the minimal unit that is matched against the tokens in the text, and a single pattern element can match to one or several tokens, depending on the pattern element type. A pattern is considered to match a sequence of tokens in the text when: first, all the PEs from the infix are matched (this gives the potential time expression mention) and, second, all the PEs from the prefix and the postfix are matched (this gives the left and right context information for the new candidate example, respectively). Therefore, patterns with a larger context window are more restrictive, because all of the PEs in the prefix and the postfix have to be matched (on top of the infix) for the pattern to yield a match.

We distinguish among token-level generalizations

```
pattern ::= prefix SEP infix SEP postfix SEP
              (modifiers)*
prefix ::= (pattern-elem)*
infix ::= (pattern-elem)+
postfix ::= (pattern-elem)*
pattern-elem ::= FORM "(" token-form ")" |
  SEMCLASS "(" token-form ")" |
  POS "(" pos-tag ")" | LEMMA "(" lemma-form ")" |
  SYN "(" syn-type "," head ")"  |
  SYN-SEM "(" syn-type "," head ")"
 modifiers ::= COMPLETE-PHRASE
```

Figure 2: The EBNF Grammar for Patterns

(i.e. PEs) and chunk-level generalizations. The former have been generated from the features of a single token and will match to a single token in the text. The latter have been generated from and match to a sequence of tokens in the text (e.g. a basic syntactic chunk). Patterns are built from the following types of PEs (which can be seen in the grammar from Figure 2):

1. Token form PEs: The more restrictive, only match a given token form.
2. Semantic class PEs: Match tokens (sometimes multiwords) that belong to a given semantic similarity class. This concept is defined below.
3. POS tag PEs: Match tokens with a given POS.
4. Lemma PEs: Match tokens with a given lemma.
5. Syntactic chunk PEs: Match a sequence of tokens that is a syntactic chunk of a given type (e.g. NP) and whose headword has the same lemma as indicated.
6. Generalized syntactic PEs: Same as the previous, but the lemma of the headword may be any in a given semantic similarity class.

The *semantic similarity class* of a word is defined as the word itself plus a group of other semantically similar words. For computing these, we employ Lin's corpus of pairwise distributional similarities among words (nouns, verbs and adjectives) (Lin, 1998), filtered to include only those words whose similarity value is above both an absolute (highest n) and relative (to the highest similarity value in the class) threshold. Even after filtering, Lin's similarities can be "noisy", since the corpus has been constructed relying on purely statistical means. Therefore, we are employing in addition a set of manually defined semantic classes (hardcoded lists) sensitive to our domain of temporal expressions, such that these lists "override" the Lin's similarity corpus whenever the semantic class of a word present in them is involved. The manually defined semantic classes include: the written form of cardinals; ordinals; days of the week (plus *today*, *tomorrow* and *yesterday*); months of the year; date trigger words (e.g. *day*, *week*); time trigger words (e.g. *hour*, *second*); frequency adverbs (e.g. *hourly*, *monthly*); date adjectives (e.g. *two- day*, *@@-week-long*); and time adjectives (e.g. *three-hour*, *@@-minute-long*).

We use a *dynamic window* for the amount of context that is encoded into a pattern, that is, we generate all the possible patterns with the same infix, and anything between 0 and the specified length of the context window PEs in the prefix and the postfix, and let the selection step decide which variations get accepted into the next iteration.

The modifiers field in the pattern representation has been devised as an extension mechanism. Currently the only implemented modifier is COMPLETE-PHRASE, which when attached to a pattern, "rounds" the instance (i.e. candidate time expression) captured by its infix to include the closest complete basic syntactic chunk (e.g. "LEMMA(end) LEMMA(of) SEMCLASS(January)" would match "the end of December 2009" instead of only "end of December" against the text "...By the end of December 2009, ..."). This modifier was implemented in view of the fact that most temporal expressions correspond with whole noun phrases or adverbial phrases.

From the above types of PEs, we have built the following types of patterns:

1. All-lemma patterns (including the prefix and postfix).
2. All-semantic class patterns.
3. Combinations of token form with sem. class.
4. Combinations of lemma with sem. class.
5. All-POS tag patterns.
6. Combinations of token form with POS tag.
7. Combinations of lemma with POS tag.
8. All-syntactic chunk patterns.
9. All-generalized syntactic patterns.

4 Ranking and selection of patterns and learning examples

4.1 Patterns

For the purposes of this section, let us define the *control set* $\mathcal{C}$ as being formed by the seed examples plus all the selected examples over the previous iterations (only the infix considered, not the context).

Note that, except for the seed examples, this is only *assumed correct*, but cannot be guaranteed to be correct (unsupervised). In addition, let us define the *instance set* $\mathcal{I}_p$ of a candidate pattern p as the set of all the instances of the pattern found in a fraction of the unlabelled corpus (only infix of the instance considered). Each candidate pattern pat is assigned two partial scores:

1. A frequency-based score $\text{freq\_sc}(\text{p})$ that measures the coverage of the pattern in (a section of) the unsupervised corpus:
   $\text{freq\_sc}(\text{p}) = \text{Card}(\mathcal{I}_p \cap \mathcal{C})$
2. A precision score $\text{prec\_sc}(\text{p})$ that evaluates the precision of the pattern in (a section of) the unsupervised corpus, measured against the control set:
   $\text{prec\_sc}(\text{p}) = \frac{\text{Card}(\mathcal{I}_p \cap \mathcal{C})}{\text{Card}(\mathcal{I}_p)}$

These two scores are computed only against a fraction of the unlabelled corpus for time efficiency. There remains an issue with whether *multisets* (counting each repeated instance several times) or *normal sets* (counting them only once) should be used for the instance sets $\mathcal{I}_p$. Our experiments indicate that the best results are obtained by employing multisets for the frequency-based score and normal sets for the precision score.

Given the two partial scores above, we have tried three different strategies for combining them:

- Multiplicative combination: $\lambda_1 \log(\epsilon_1 + \text{freq\_sc}(\text{p})) + \lambda_2 \log(\epsilon_2 + \text{prec\_sc}(\text{p}))$
- The strategy suggested in (Collins and Singer, 1999): Patterns are first filtered by imposing a threshold on their precision score. Only for those patterns that pass this first filter, their final score is considered to be their frequency-based score.
- The strategy suggested in (Riloff, 1996):
  $\begin{cases} \text{prec\_sc}(\text{p}) \cdot \log(\text{freq\_sc}(\text{p})) & \text{if prec\_sc}(\text{p}) \geq \text{thr} \\ 0 & \text{otherwise} \end{cases}$

4.1.1 Analysis of subsumptions

Intertwined with the selection step, an analysis of subsumptions is performed among the selected patterns, and the patterns found to be subsumed by others in the set are discarded. This is repeated until either a maximum of m patterns with no subsumptions among them are selected, or the list of candidate patterns is exhausted, whichever happens first. The purpose of this analysis of subsumptions is twofold: on the one hand, it results in a cleaner output pattern set by getting rid of redundant patterns; on the other hand, it improves temporal efficiency by reducing the number of patterns being handled in the last step of the algorithm (i.e. searching for new candidate examples).

In our scenario, a pattern p_1 with instance set $\mathcal{I}_{p_1}$ is subsumed by a pattern p_2 with instance set $\mathcal{I}_{p_2}$ if $\mathcal{I}_{p_1} \subset \mathcal{I}_{p_2}$. We make a distinction among "theoretical" and "empirical" subsumptions. Theoretical subsumptions are those that can be justified based on theoretical grounds alone, from observing the form of the patterns. Empirical subsumptions are those cases where in fact one pattern subsumes another according to the former definition, but this could only be detected by having calculated their respective instance sets a priori, which beats one of the purposes of the analysis of subsumptions —namely, temporal efficiency—. We are only dealing with theoretical subsumptions here. A pattern *theoretically subsumes* another pattern when either of these conditions occur:

- The first pattern is identical to the second, except that the first has fewer contextual PEs in the prefix and/or the postfix.
- Part or all of the PEs of the first pattern are identical to the corresponding PEs in the second pattern, except for the fact that they are of a *more general type* (element-wise); the remaining PEs are identical. To this end, we have defined a partial order of generality in the PE types (see section 3), as follows:
  FORM $\prec$ LEMMA $\prec$ SEMCLASS; FORM $\prec$ POS;
  SYN $\prec$ SYN-SEMC
- Both the above conditions (fewer contextual PEs and of a more general type) happen at the same time.

4.2 Learning Examples

An *example* is composed of the tokens which have been identified as a potential time expression (which we shall call the *infix*) plus a certain amount of left and right context (from now on, the *context*) encoded alongside the infix. For ranking and selecting examples, we first assign a score and select a number n of distinct *infixes* and, in a second stage, we assign a score to each context of appearance of an infix and select (at most) m contexts per infix. Our scoring system for the infixes is adapted from (Paşca et al., 2006). Each distinct infix receives three partial scores and the final score for the infix is a linear combination of these, with the λ_i being parameters: $\lambda_1 \text{sim\_sc(ex)} + \lambda_2 \text{pc\_sc(ex)} + \lambda_3 \text{ctxt\_sc(ex)}$

1. A similarity-based score (sim_sc(ex)), which measures the semantic similarity (as per the Lin's similarity corpus (Lin, 1998)) of the infix with respect to set of "accepted" output examples from all previous iterations plus the initial seeds. If $w_1, \ldots, w_n$ are the tokens in the infix (excluding stopwords); $e_{j,1}, \ldots, e_{j,m_j}$ are the tokens in the j-th example of the set E of seed plus output examples; and $\text{sv}(x, y)$ represents a similarity value, the similarity $\text{Sim}(w_i)$ of the i-th word of the infix wrt the seeds and output is given by $\text{Sim}(w_i) = \sum_{j=1}^{|E|} \max(\text{sv}(w_i, e_{j,1}), \ldots, \text{sv}(w_i, e_{j,m_j}))$, and the similarity-based score of an infix containing n words is given by $\frac{\sum_{i=1}^{n} \log(1+\text{Sim}(w_i))}{n}$.
2. A phrase-completeness score (pc_sc(ex)), which measures the likelihood that the infix is a complete time expression and not merely a part of one, over the entire set of candidate example: $\frac{\text{count(INFIX)}}{\text{count(*INFIX*)}}$
3. A context-based score (ctxt_sc(ex)), intended as a measure of the infix's relevance. For each context (up to a length) where this infix appears in the corpus, the frequency of the word with maximum relative frequency (over the words in all the infix's contexts) is taken. The sum is then scaled by the relative frequency of this particular infix.

Apart from the score associated with the infix, each example (i.e. infix plus a context) receives two additional frequency scores for the left and right context part of the example respectively. Each of these is given by the relative frequency of the token with maximum frequency of that context, computed over all the tokens that appear in all the contexts of all the candidate examples. For each selected infix, the m contexts with best score are selected.

5 Experiments

5.1 Experimental setup

As unsupervised data for our experiments, we use the NW (newswire) category of LDC's ACE 2005 Unsupervised Data Pool, containing 456 Mbytes of data in 204K documents for a total of over 82 million tokens. Simultaneously, we use a much smaller labelled corpus (where the correct time expressions are tagged) to measure the precision, recall and F_1-measure of the pattern set learned by the bootstrapping process. This is the ACE 2005 corpus, containing 550 documents with 257K tokens and approx. 4650 time expression mentions. The labelled corpus is split in two halves: one half is used to obtain the initial *seed examples* from among the time expressions found therein; the other half is used for evaluation. We are requiring that a pattern captures the target time expression mention *exactly* (no misalignment allowed at the boundaries), in order to count it as a precision or recall hit.

We will also be interested in measuring the *gain in recall*, that is, the difference between the recall in the best iteration and the initial recall given by the seeds. Also important is the number of iterations after which the bootstrapping process converges. In the case where the same F_1- measure mark is achieved in two experimental settings, earlier convergence of the algorithm will be prefered. Otherwise, better F_1 and gain in recall are the primary goals.

In order to start with a set of seeds with high precision, we select them automatically, imposing that a seed time expression must have precision above a certain value (understood as the percentage, of all the appearances of the sequence of tokens in the supervised corpus, those in which it is tagged as a correct time expression). In the experiments presented below, this threshold for precision of the seeds is 90% —in the half of the supervised corpus reserved for extraction of seeds—. From those that pass this filter, the ones that appear with greater frequency are selected. For time expressions that have an identical digit pattern (e.g. two dates "@@ December" or two years "@@@@", where @ stands for any digit), only one seed is taken. This approach simulates the human domain expert, which typically is the first step in bootstrapping IE models

Unless specifically stated otherwise, all the experiments presented below share the following default settings:

- Only the first 2.36 Mbytes of the unsupervised corpus are used (10 Mbytes after tokenization and feature extraction), that is 0.5% of the available data. This is to keep the execution time of experiments low, where multiple experiments need to be run to optimize a certain parameter.
- We use the Collins and Singer strategy (see section 4.1) with a precision threshold of 0.50 for sub-score combination in pattern selection. This strategy favours patterns with slightly higher precision.
- The maximum length of prefix and postfix is 1 and 0 elements, respectively. This was determined experimentally.
- 100 seed examples are used (out of a maximum of 605 available).
- In the ranking of examples, the λ_i weights for the three sub- scores for infixes are 0.5 for the "similarity-based score", 0.25 for "phrase-completeness" and 0.25 for "context-based score".
- In the selection of examples, the maximum number of new infixes accepted per iteration is 200, with a maximum of 50 different contexts per infix. In the selection of patterns, the maximum number of new accepted patterns per iteration is 5000 (although this number is never reached due to the analysis of subsumptions).
- In the selection of patterns, multisets are used for computing the instance set of a pattern for the frequency-based score and normal sets for the precision score (determined experimentally).
- The POS tag type of generalization (pattern element) has been deactivated, that is, neither all-POS patterns, nor patterns that are combinations of POS PEs with another are generated. After an analysis of errors, it was observed that POS generalizations (because of the fact that they are not lexicalized like, for instance, the syntactic PEs with a given headword) give rise to a considerable number of precision errors.
- All patterns are generated with COMPLETE-PHRASE modifier automatically attached. It was determined experimentally that it was best to use this heuristic in all cases (see section 3).

5.2 Variation of the number of seeds

We have performed experiments using 1, 5, 10, 20, 50, 100, 200 and 500 seeds. The general trends observed were as follows. The final precision (when the bootstrapping converges) decreases more or less monotonically as the number of seeds increases, although there are slight fluctuations; besides, the difference in this respect between using few seeds (20 to 50) or more (100 to 200) is of only around 3%. However, a big leap can be observed in moving from 200 to 500 seeds, where both the initial precision (of the seeds) and final precision (at point of convergence) drop by 10% wrt to using 200 seeds. The final recall increases monotonically as the number of seeds increases —since more supervised information is provided—. The final F_1-measure first increases and then decreases with an increasing number of seeds, with an optimum value being reached somewhere between the 50 and 100 seeds.

The largest gain in recall (difference between recall of the seeds and recall at the point of convergence) is achieved with 20 seeds, for a gain of 16.38% (initial recall is 20.08% and final is 36.46%). The best mark in F_1-measure is achieved with 100 seeds, after 6 iterations: 60.43% (the final precision is 69.29% and the final recall is 53.58%; the drop in precision is 6.5% and the gain in recall is 14.28%). Figure 3 shows a line plot of precision vs recall for these experiments. This experiment suggests that the problem of temporal expression recognition can be captured with minimal supervised information (100 seeds) and larger amounts of unsupervised information.

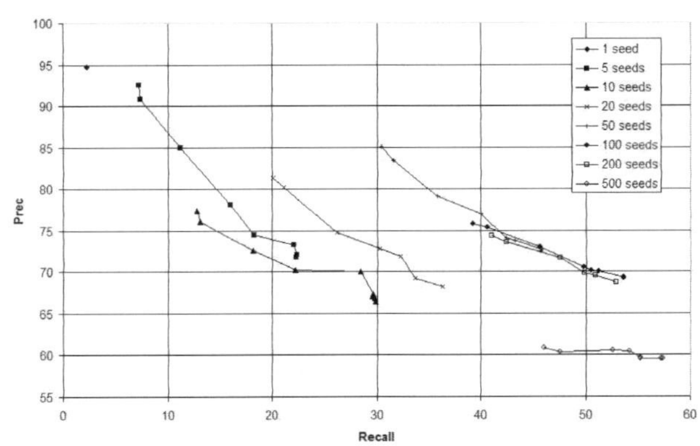

Figure 3: Effect of varying the number of seeds

5.3 Variation of the type of generalizations used in patterns

In these experiments, we have defined four differents sets of generalizations (i.e. types of pattern elements among those specified in section 3) to evaluate how semantic and syntactic generalizations contribute to performance of the algorithm. These four experiments are labelled as follows: NONE includes only PEs of the LEMMA type; SYN includes PEs of the lemma type and of the not-generalized syntactic chunk (SYN) type; SEM includes PEs of the lemma type and of the semantic class (SEMCLASS) type, as well as combinations of lemma with SEMCLASS PEs; and lastly, SYN+SEM includes everything that both SYN and SEM experiments include, plus PEs of the generalized syntactic chunk (SYNSEMC) type.

One can observe than neither type of generalization, syntactic or semantic, is specially "effective" when used in isolation (only a 3.5% gain in recall in both cases). It is only the combination of both types that gives a good gain in recall (14.28% in the case of this experiment). Figure 4 shows a line plot of this experiment. The figure indicates that the problem of temporal expression recognition, even though apparently simple, requires both syntactic and semantic information for efficient modeling.

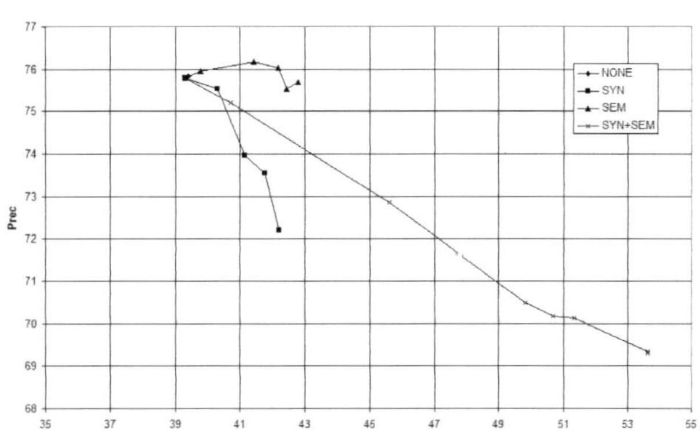

Figure 4: Effect of using syntactic and/or semantic generalizations

5.4 Variation of the size of unsupervised data used

We performed experiments using increasing amounts of unsupervised data for training in the bootstrapping: 1, 5, 10, 50 and 100 Mbytes of preprocessed corpus (tokenized and with feature extraction). The amounts of plain text data are roughly a fifth part, respectively. The objective of these experiments is to determine whether performance improves as the amount of training data is increased. The number of seeds passed to the bootstrapping is 68. The maximum number of new infixes (the part of an example that contains a candidate time expression) accepted per iteration has been increased from 200 to 1000, because it was observed that larger amounts of unsupervised training data need a greater number of selection "slots" in order to render an improvement (that is, a more "reckless" bootstrapping), otherwise they will fill up all the allowed selection slots.

The observed effect is that both the drop in precision (from the initial iteration to the point of convergence) and the gain in recall improve more or less consistently as a larger amount of training data is taken, or otherwise the same recall point is achieved in an earlier iteration. These improvements are nevertheless slight, in the order of between 0.5% and 2%. The biggest improvement is observed in the 100 Mbytes experiment, where recall after 5 iterations is 6% better than in the 50 Mbytes experiment after 7 iterations. The drop in precision in the 100 Mbytes experiment is 13.05%, for a gain in recall of 21.36% (final precision is 71.02%, final recall 52.84% and final F_1 60.59%). Figure 5 shows a line plot of this experiment. This experiment indicates that increasing amounts of unsupervised data can be used to improve the performance of our model, but the task is not trivial.

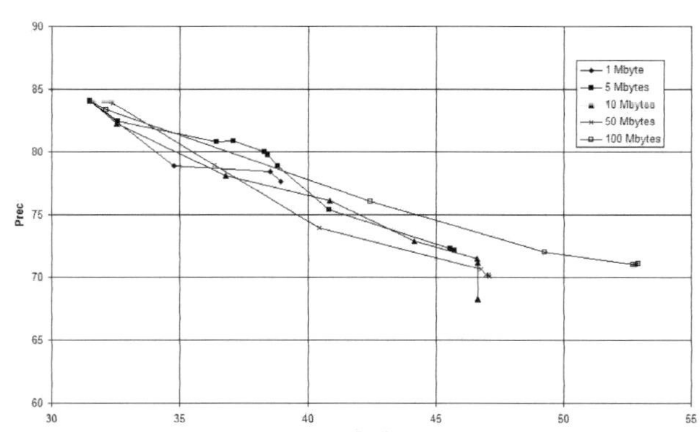

Figure 5: Effect of varying the amount of unsupervised training data

6 Conclusions and future research

We have presented a slightly supervised algorithm for the extraction of IE patterns for the recognition of time expressions, based on bootstrapping, which introduces a novel representation of patterns suited to this task. Our experiments show that with a relatively small amount of supervision (50 to 100 initial correct examples or seeds) and using a combination of syntactic and semantic generalizations, it is possible to obtain an improvement of around 15%-20% in recall (with regard to the seeds) and F_1-measure over 60% learning exclusively from unlabelled data. Furthermore, using increasing amounts of unlabelled training data (of which there is plenty available) is a workable way to obtain small improvements in performance, at the expense of training time. Our current focus is on addressing specific problems that appear on inspection of the precision errors in test, which can improve both precision and recall to a degree. Future planned lines of research include using WordNet for improving the semantic aspects of the algorithm (semantic classes and similarity), and studying forms of combining the patterns obtained in this semi-supervised approach with supervised learning.

References

M. Collins and Y. Singer. 1999. Unsupervised models for named entity classification. In *Proceedings of the Joint SIGDAT Conference on Empirical Methods in Natural Language Processing and Very Large Corpora*, pages 100–110, College Park, MD. ACL.

L. Ferro, L. Gerber, I. Mani, B. Sundheim, and G. Wilson. 2005. Tides 2005 standard for the annotation of temporal expressions. Technical report, MITRE Corporation.

E. Filatova and E. Hovy. 2001. Assigning time-stamps to event-clauses. In *Proceedings of the 2001 ACL Workshop on Temporal and Spatial Information Processing*, pages 88–95.

K. Hacioglu, Y. Chen, and B. Douglas. 2005. Automatic time expression labelling for english and chinese text. In *Proc. of the 6th International Conference on Intelligent Text Processing and Computational Linguistics (CICLing)*, pages 548–559. Springer.

Z. Kozareva, E. Riloff, and E. Hovy. 2008. Semantic class learning from the web with hyponym pattern linkage graphs. In *Proc. of the Association for Computational Linguistics 2008 (ACL-2008:HLT)*, pages 1048–1056.

D. Lin. 1998. Automatic retrieval and clustering of similar words. In *Proceedings of the 17th International Conference on Computational Linguistics and the 36th Annual Meeting of the Association for Computational Linguistics (COLING-ACL-98)*, pages 768–774, Montreal, Quebec. ACL.

I. Mani and G. Wilson. 2000. Robust temporal processing of news. In *Proceedings of the 38th Annual Meeting of the Association for Computational Linguistics*, pages 69–76, Morristown, NJ, USA. ACL.

M. Paşca, D. Lin, J. Bigham, A. Lifchits, and A. Jain. 2006. Names and similarities on the web: Fact extraction in the fast lane. In *Proceedings of the 21th International Conference on Computational Linguistics and 44th Annual Meeting of the ACL*, pages 809–816. ACL.

E. Riloff. 1996. Automatically generating extraction patterns from untagged text. In *Proceedings of the Thirteenth National Conference on Artificial Intelligence (AAAI-96)*, pages 1044–1049. AAAI/MIT Press.

E. Saquete, R. Muñoz, and P. Martínez-Barco. 2004. Event ordering using terseo system. In *Proc. of the 9th International Conference on Application of Natural Language to Information Systems (NLDB)*, pages 39–50. Springer.

M. Stevenson and M. Greenwood. 2005. A semantic approach to IE pattern induction. In *Proceedings of the 43rd Meeting of the Association for Computational Linguistics*, pages 379–386. ACL.

M. Surdeanu, J. Turmo, and A. Ageno. 2006. A hybrid approach for the acquisition of information extraction patterns. In *Proceedings of the EACL 2006 Workshop on Adaptive Text Extraction and Mining (ATEM 2006)*. ACL.

J. M. Wiebe, T. P. O'Hara, T. Ohrstrom-Sandgren, and K. J. McKeever. 1998. An empirical approach to temporal reference resolution. *Journal of Artificial Intelligence Research*, 9:247–293.

R. Yangarber, R. Grishman, P. Tapanainen, and S. Hutunen. 2000. Automatic acquisition of domain knowledge for information extraction. In *Proceedings of the 18th International Conference of Computational Linguistics*, pages 940–946.

R. Yangarber. 2003. Counter-training in discovery of semantic patterns. In *Proceedings of the 41st Annual Meeting of the Association for Computational Linguistics*. ACL.

D. Yarowsky. 1995. Unsupervised word sense disambiguation rivaling supervised methods. In *Proceedings of the 33rd Annual Meeting of the Association for Computational Linguistics*, pages 189–196, Cambridge, MA. ACL.

A Simple Semi-supervised Algorithm For Named Entity Recognition

Wenhui Liao and Sriharsha Veeramachaneni
Research and Develpment,Thomson Reuters
610 Opperman Drive, Eagan MN 55123
{wenhui.liao, harsha.veeramachaneni}@thomsonreuters.com

Abstract

We present a simple semi-supervised learning algorithm for named entity recognition (NER) using conditional random fields (CRFs). The algorithm is based on exploiting evidence that is independent from the features used for a classifier, which provides high-precision labels to unlabeled data. Such independent evidence is used to automatically extract high-accuracy and non-redundant data, leading to a much improved classifier at the next iteration. We show that our algorithm achieves an average improvement of 12 in recall and 4 in precision compared to the supervised algorithm. We also show that our algorithm achieves high accuracy when the training and test sets are from different domains.

1 Introduction

Named entity recognition (NER) or tagging is the task of finding names such as organizations, persons, locations, etc. in text. Since whether or not a word is a name and the entity type of a name are determined mostly by the context of the word as well as by the entity type of its neighbors, NER is often posed as a sequence classification problem and solved by methods such as hidden Markov models (HMM) and conditional random fields (CRF).

Automatically tagging named entities (NE) with high precision and recall requires a large amount of hand-annotated data, which is expensive to obtain. This problem presents itself time and again because tagging the same NEs in different domains usually requires different labeled data. However, in most domains one often has access to large amounts of unlabeled text. This fact motivates semi-supervised approaches for NER.

Semi-supervised learning involves the utilization of unlabeled data to mitigate the effect of insufficient labeled data on classifier accuracy. One variety of semi-supervised learning essentially attempts to automatically generate high-quality training data from an unlabeled corpus. Algorithms such as co-training (Blum and Mitchell, 1998)(Collins and Singer, 1999)(Pierce and Cardie, 2001) and the Yarowsky algorithm (Yarowsky, 1995) make assumptions about the data that permit such an approach.

The main requirement for the automatically generated training data in addition to high accuracy, is that it covers regions in the feature space with low probability density. Furthermore, it is necessary that all the classes are represented according to their prior probabilities in every region in the feature space. One approach to achieve these goals is to select unlabeled data that has been classified with low confidence by the classifier trained on the original training data, but whose labels are known with high precision from *independent* evidence. Here independence means that the high-precision *decision rule* that classifies these low confidence instances uses information that is independent of the features used by the classifier.

We propose two ways of obtaining such independent evidence for NER. The first is based on the fact that multiple mentions of capitalized tokens are likely to have the same label and occur in independently chosen contexts. We call this the

Proceedings of the NAACL HLT Workshop on Semi-supervised Learning for Natural Language Processing, pages 58–65,
Boulder, Colorado, June 2009.

multi-mention property. The second is based on the fact that entities such as organizations, persons, etc., have context that is highly indicative of the class, yet is independent of the other context (e.g. company suffixes like Inc., Co., etc., person titles like Mr., CEO, etc.). We call such context *high precision independent context.*

Let us first look at two examples.

Example 1:

1) said Harry You, CEO of HearingPoint ....

2) For this year's second quarter, You said the company's ...

The classifier tags "Harry You" as person (*PER*) correctly since its context (said, CEO) makes it an obvious name. However, in the second sentence, the classifier fails to tag "You" as a person since "You" is usually a stopword. The second sentence is exactly the type of data needed in the training set.

Example 2:

(1) Medtronic Inc 4Q profits rise 10 percent...

(2) Medtronic 4Q profits rise 10 percent...

The classifier tags "Medtronic" correctly in the first sentence because of the company suffix "Inc" while it fails to tag "Medtronic" in the second sentence since "4Q profits" is a new pattern and "Medtronic" is unseen in the training data. Thus the second sentence is what we need in the training set.

The two examples have one thing in common. In both cases, the second sentence has a new pattern and incorrect labels, which can be fixed by using either multi-mention or high-precision context from the first sentence. We actually *artificially* construct the second sentence to be added to the training set in Example 2 although only the first sentence exists in the unlabeled corpus.

By leveraging such independent evidence, our algorithm can automatically extract high-accuracy and non-redundant data for training, and thus obtain an improved model for NER. Specifically, our algorithm starts with a model trained with a small amount of gold data (manually tagged data). This model is then used to extract high-confidence data, which is then used to discover low-confidence data by using other independent features. These low-confidence data are then added to the training data to retrain the model. The whole process repeats until no significant improvement can be achieved. Our experiments show that the algorithm is not only much better than the initial model, but also better than the supervised learning when a large amount of gold data are available. Especially, even when the domain from which the original training data is sampled is different from the domain of the testing data, our algorithm still provides significant gains in classification accuracy.

2 Related Work

The Yarowsky algorithm (Yarowsky, 1995), originally proposed for word sense disambiguation, makes the assumption that it is very unlikely for two occurrences of a word in the same discourse to have different senses. This assumption is exploited by selecting words classified with high confidence according to sense and adding other contexts of the same words in the same discourse to the training data, even if they have low confidence. This allows the algorithm to learn new contexts for the senses leading to higher accuracy. Our algorithm also uses multi-mention features. However, the application of the Yarowsky algorithm to NER involves several domain-specific choices as will become evident below.

Wong and Ng (Wong and Ng, 2007) use the same idea of multiple mentions of a token sequence being to the same named entity for feature engineering. They use a named entity recognition model based on the maximum entropy framework to tag a large unlabeled corpus. Then the majority tags of the named entities are collected in lists. The model is then retrained by using these lists as extra features. This method requires a sufficient amount of manually tagged data initially to work. Their paper shows that, if the initial model has a low F-score, the model with the new features leads to low F-score too. Our method works with a small amount of gold data because, instead of constructing new features, we use independent evidence to enrich the training data with high-accuracy and non-redundant data.

The co-training algorithm proposed by Blum and Mitchell (Blum and Mitchell, 1998) assumes that the features can be split into two class-conditionally independent sets or "views" and that each view is sufficient for accurate classification. The classifier built on *one* of the views is used to classify a large unlabeled corpus and the data classified with high-confidence are added to the training set on which the classifier on the *other* view is trained. This process is iterated by interchanging the views. The main reason that co-training works is that, because of the class-conditional independence assumptions, the high-confidence data from one view, in addition to being highly precise, is unbiased when added to the training set for the other view. We could not apply co-training for semi-supervised named entity recognition because of the difficulty of finding informative yet class-conditionally independent feature sets.

Collins et al.(Collins and Singer, 1999) proposed two algorithms for NER by modifying Yarowsky's method (Yarowsky, 1995) and the framework suggested by (Blum and Mitchell, 1998). However, all their features are at the word sequence level, instead of at the token level. At the token level, the seed rules they proposed do not necessarily work. In addition, parsing sentences into word sequences is not a trivial task, and also not necessary for NER, in our opinion.

Jiao et al. propose semi-supervised conditional random fields (Jiao et al., 2006) that try to maximize the conditional log-likelihood on the training data and simultaneously minimize the conditional entropy of the class labels on the unlabeled data. This approach is reminiscent of the semi-supervised learning algorithms that try to discourage the boundary from being in regions with high density of unlabeled data. The resulting objective function is no longer convex and may result in local optima. Our approach in contrast avoids changing the CRF training procedure, which guarantees global maximum.

3 Named Entity Recognition

As long as independent evidence exists for one type of NE, our method can be directly applied to classify such NE. As an example, we demonstrate how to apply our method to classify three types of NEs: organization (ORG), person (PER), and location (LOC) since they are the most common ones. A non-NE is annotated as O.

3.1 Conditional Random Fields for NER

We use CRF to perform classification in our framework. CRFs are undirected graphical models trained to maximize the conditional probability of a sequence of labels given the corresponding input sequence. Let X, $X = x_1...x_N$, be an input sequence, and Y, $Y = y_1....y_N$, be the label sequence for the input sequence. The conditional probability of Y given X is:

$$P(Y|X) = \frac{1}{Z(X)} \exp(\sum_{n=1}^{N} \sum_{k} \lambda_k f_k(y_{n-1}, y_n, X, n)) \tag{1}$$

where $Z(X)$ is a normalization term, f_k is a feature function, which often takes a binary value, and λ_k is a learned weight associated with the feature f_k. The parameters can be learned by maximizing log-likelihood ℓ which is given by

$$\ell = \sum_{i} \log P(Y_i|X_i) - \sum_{k} \frac{\lambda_k^2}{2\sigma_k^2} \tag{2}$$

where σ_k^2 is the smoothing (or regularization) parameter for feature f_k. The penalty term, used for regularization, basically imposes a prior distribution on the parameters.

It has been shown that ℓ is convex and thus a global optimum is guaranteed (McCallum, 2003). Inferring label sequence for an input sequence X involves finding the most probable label sequence, $Y^* = \arg\max_{Y} P(Y|X)$, which is done by the Viterbi algorithm (Forney, 1973).

3.2 Features for NER

One big advantage of CRF is that it can naturally represent rich domain knowledge with features.

3.2.1 Standard Features

Part of the features we used for our CRF classifier are common features that are widely used in NER (McCallum and Li, 2003), as shown below.

1) *Lexicon*. Each token is itself a feature.

2) *Orthography*. Orthographic information is used to identify whether a token is capitalized, or an acronym, or a pure number, or a punctuation, or has mixed letters and digits, etc.

3) *Single/multiple-token list*. Each list is a collection of words that have a common sematic meaning, such as last name, first name, organization, company suffix, city, university, etc.

4) *Joint features.* Joint features are the conjunctions of individual features. For example, if a token is in a last name list and its previous token is in a title list, the token will have a joint feature called as Title+Name.

5) *Features of neighbors.* After extracting the above features for each token, its features are then copied to its neighbors (The neighbors of a token include the previous two and next two tokens) with a position id. For example, if the previous token of a token has a feature "Cap@0", this token will have a feature "Cap@-1".

3.2.2 Label Features

One unique and important feature used in our algorithm is called *Label Features*. A label feature is the output label of a token itself if it is known. We designed some simple high-precision rules to classify each token, which take precedence over the CRF. Specifically, if a token does not include any uppercase letter, is not a number, and it is not in the *nocap* list (which includes the tokens that are not capitalized but still could be part of an NE, such as al, at, in, -, etc), the label of this token is "O".

Table 1: An example of extracted features

Tokens	Feature
Monday	W=Monday@0 O@0
vice	W=vice@0 O@0
chairman	W=chairman@0 title@0 O@0
Goff	W=Goff@0 CAP@0 Lastname@0 W=chairman@-1 title@-1 O@-1 W=vice@-2 O@-2 W=said@1 O@1 W=it@2 O@2
said	W=said@0 O@0
the	W=it@0 O@0
company	W=company@0 O@0

In addition, if a token is surrounded by "O" tokens and is in a *Stopword* list, or in a *Time* list (a collection of date, time related tokens), or in a *nocap* list, or a *nonNE* list (a collection of tokens that are unlikely to be an NE), or a pure number, its label is "O" as well. For example, in the sentence "Ford has said there is no plan to lay off workers", all the tokens except "Ford" have "O" labels. More rules can be designed to classify NE labels. For example, if a token is in an unambiguousORG list, it has a label "ORG".

For any token with a known label, unless it is a neighbor of a token with its label unknown (i.e., not pretagged with high precision), its features include only its lexicon and its label itself. No features will be copied from its neighbors either. Table 1 gives an example to demonstrate the features used in our algorithm. For the sentence "Monday vice chairman Goff said the company ...", only "Goff" includes its own features and features copied from its neighbors, while most of the other tokens have only two features since they are "O" tokens based on the high-precision rules.

Usually, more than half the tokens will be classified as "O". This strategy greatly saves feature extraction time, training time, and inference time, as well as improving the accuracy of the model. Most importantly, this strategy is necessary in the semi-supervised learning, which will be explained in the next section.

4 Semi-supervised Learning Algorithm

Our semi-supervised algorithm is outlined in Table 2. We assume that we have a small amount of labeled data L and a classifier C_k that is trained on L. We exploit a large unlabeled corpus U from the test domain from which we automatically and gradually add new training data D to L, such that L has two properties: 1) *accurately labeled*, meaning that the labels assigned by automatic annotation of the selected unlabeled data are correct, and 2) *non-redundant*, which means that the new data is from regions in the feature space that the original training set does not adequately cover. Thus the classifier C_k is expected to get better monotonically as the training data gets updated.

Table 2: The semi-supervised NER algorithm

Given:
- L - a small set of labeled training data
- U - unlabeled data

Loop for k iterations:
- Step 1: Train a classifier C_k based on L;
- Step 2: Extract new data D based on C_k;
- Step 3: Add D to L;

At each iteration, the classifier trained on the previous training data (using the features introduced in the previous section) is used to tag the unlabeled data. In addition, for each O token and NE segment, a confidence score is computed using the constrained forward-backward algorithm (Culotta and McCallum, 2004), which calculates the L_X^c, the sum of the probabilities of all the paths passing through the constrained segment (constrained to be the assigned labels).

One way to increase the size of the training data is to add all the tokens classified with high confidence to the training set. This scheme is unlikely to improve the accuracy of the classifier at the next iteration because the newly added data is unlikely to include new patterns. Instead, we use the high confidence data to tag other data by exploiting independent features.

- Tagging ORG

  If a sequence of tokens has been classified as "ORG" with high confidence score ($> T$)[1], we force the labels of other occurrences of the same sequence in the same document, to be "ORG" and add all such duplicate sequences classified with low confidence to the training data for the next iteration. In addition if a high confidence segment ends with company suffix, we remove the company suffix and check the multi-mentions of the remaining segment also. In addition to that, we reclassify the sentence after removing the company suffix and check if the labels are still the same with high-confidence. If not, the sequence will be added to the training data. As shown in Example 4, "Safeway shares ticked" is added to training data because "Safeway" has low confidence after removing "Inc.".

  Example 4:
  High-confidence ORG: ***Safeway Inc.*** *shares ticked up ...*
  Low-confidence ORG:
  1) ***Safeway*** *shares ticked up ...*
  2) Wall Street expects ***Safeway*** *to post earnings ...*

- Tagging PER

  If a PER segment has a high confidence score and includes at least two tokens, both this segment and the last token of this segment are used to find their other mentions. Similarly, we force their labels to be PER and add them to the training data if their confidence score is low. However, if these mentions are followed by any company suffix and are not classified as ORG, their labels, as well as the company suffix are forced to be ORG (e.g., Jefferies & Co.). We require the high-confidence PER segment to include at least two tokens because the classifier may confuse single-token ORG with PER due to their common context. For example, "Tesoro proposed 1.63 billion purchase of...", *Tesoro* has high-confidence based on the model, but it represents *Tesoro Corp* in the document and thus is an ORG.

  In addition, the title feature can be used similarly as the company suffix features. If a PER with a title feature has a high confidence score, but has a low score after the title feature is removed, the PER and its neighbors will be put into training data after removing the title-related tokens.

  Example 5:
  High-confidence PER:
  1)Investor AB appoints ***Johan Bygge*** *as CFO...*
  2)He is replacing Chief CEO ***Avallone****...*
  Low-confidence PER:
  1) ***Bygge*** *is employed at...*
  2) He is replacing ***Avallone*** *...*
  (It is obvious for a human-being that Bygge is PER because of the existence of "employed". However, when the training data doesn't include such cases, the classifier just cannot recognize it.)

- Tagging LOC

  The same approach is used for a LOC segment with a high confidence score. We force the labels of its other mentions to be LOC and add them to the training data if their confidence score is low. Again, if any of these mentions follows or is followed by an ORG segment with a high confidence score, we force the labels to be ORG as well. This is because when a LOC is around an ORG, the LOC is usually treated as part of an ORG, e.g., Google China.

[1]Through the rest of the paper, a high confidence score means the score is larger than T. In our experiments, T is set as 0.98. A low confidence score means the score is lower than 0.8.

Example 6:
High-confidence LOC: The former Soviet republic of **Azerbaijan** *is...*
Low-confidence PER:
Azerbaijan *energy reserves better than...*
Change LOC to ORG: shareholders of the ***Chicago Board of Trade...***

- Tagging O

  Since all the NE segments added to the training data have low confidence scores based on the original model, and especially since many of them were incorrectly classified before correction, these segments form good training data candidates. However, all of them are positive examples. To balance the training data, we need negative examples as well. If a token is classified as "O" with high confidence score and does not have a label feature "O", this token will be used as a negative example to be added to the training data.

Since the features of each token include the features copied from its neighbors, in addition to those extracted from the token itself, its neighbors need to be added to the training set also. If the confidence of the neighbors are low, the neighbors will be removed from the training data after copying their features to the token of interest. If the confidence scores of the neighbors are high, we further extend to the neighbors of the neighbors until low-confidence tokens are reached. We remove low-confidence neighbors in order to reduce the chances of adding training examples with false labels.

Table 3: Step 2 of the semi-supervised algorithm

Step 2: Extract new data D based on C_k
i) Classify kth portion of U and compute confidence scores;
ii) Find high-confidence NE segments and use them to tag other low-confidence tokens
iii) Find qualified O tokens
iv) Extract selected NE and O tokens as well as their neighbors
v) Shuffle part of the NEs in the extracted data
vi) Add extracted data to D

Now we have both negative and positive training examples. However, one problem with the positive data is that the same NE may appear too many times since the multi-mention property is used. For example, the word "Citigroup" may appear hundreds of times in recent financial articles because of the subprime crisis. To account for this bias in the data we randomly replace these NEs. Specifically, we replace a portion of such NEs with NEs randomly chosen from our NE lists. The size of the portion is decided by the ratio of the NEs that are not in our NE list over all the NEs in the gold data.

Table 3 summarizes the key sub-steps in Step 2 of the algorithm. At each step, more non-redundant and high-accuracy data is added into the training set and thus improves the model gradually.

5 Experiments

The data set used in the experiments is explained in Table 4. Although we have 1000 labeled news documents from the Thomson Financial (TF) News source, only 60 documents are used as the initial training data in our algorithm. For the evaluation, the gold data was split into training and test sets as appropriate. The toolbox we used for CRF is Mallet (McCallum, 2002).

Table 4: Data source. Tokens include words, punctuation and sentence breaks.

Gold Data	1000 docs from TF news (around 330 tokens per doc)
Unlabeled Corpus	100,000 docs from TF news

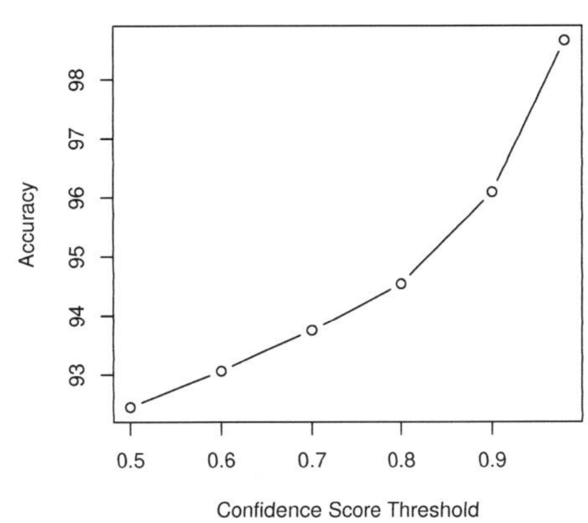

Figure 1: Token accuracy vs confidence score.

We first investigated our assumption that a high confidence score indicates high classification accuracy. Figure 1 illustrates how accuracy varies as CRF confidence score changes when 60 documents are used as training data and the remaining are used as testing data. When the threshold is 0.98, the token accuracy is close to 99%. We believe this accuracy is sufficiently high to justify using the high confidence score to extract tokens with correct labels.

Table 5: Precision and recall of the automatically extracted training data

NE	Precision%	Recall%	F-score%
LOC	94.5	96.8	95.6
ORG	96.6	93.4	94.9
PER	95.0	89.6	92.2

We wished to study the accuracy of our training data generation strategy from how well it does on the gold data. We treat the remaining gold data (except the data trained for the initial model) as if they were unlabeled, and then applied our data extraction strategy on them. Table 5 illustrates the precision and recall for the three types of NEs of the extracted data, which only accounts for a small part of the gold data. The average F-score is close to 95%. Although the precision and recall are not perfect, we believe they are good enough for the training purpose, considering that human tagged data is seldom more accurate.

We compared the semi-supervised algorithm with a supervised algorithm using the same features. The semi-supervised algorithm starts with 60 labeled documents (around 20,000 tokens) and ends with around 1.5 million tokens. We trained the supervised algorithm with two data sets: using only 60 documents (around 20,000 tokens) and using 700 documents (around 220,000 tokens) respectively. The reason for the choice of the training set size is the fact that 20,000 tokens are a reasonably small amount of data for human to tag, and 220,000 tokens are the amount usually used for supervised algorithms (CoNLL 2003 English NER (Sang and Meulder, 2003) training set has around 220,000 tokens).

Table 6 illustrates the results when 300 documents are used for testing. As shown in Table 6, starting with only 6% of the gold data, the semi-supervised algorithm achieves much better results than the semi-supervised algorithm when the same amount of gold data is used. For LOC, ORG, and PER, the recall increases 5.5, 16.8, and 8.2 respectively, and the precision increases 2.4, 1.5, and 6.8 respectively. Even compared with the model trained with 220,000 tokens, the semi-supervised learning algorithm is better. Especially, for PER, the precision and recall increase 2.8 and 4.6 respectively. Figure 2 illustrates how the classifier is improved at each iteration in the semi-supervised learning algorithm.

Table 6: Classification results. P/R represents Precision/Recall. The numbers inside the parentheses are the result differences when the model trained from 60 docs is used as baseline.

Training Data	P/R(LOC)	P/R(ORG)	P/R(PER)
60 docs	88.1/85.6	86.0/64.2	74.5/81.2
700 docs	91.2/88.2	90.5/76.6	78.3/84.8
	(3.1/3.6)	(4.5/12.4)	(3.8/3.6)
semi-supervised	90.5/91.1	87.5/81.0	81.1/89.4
(60 docs)	**(2.4/5.5)**	**(1.5/16.8)**	**(6.6/8.2)**

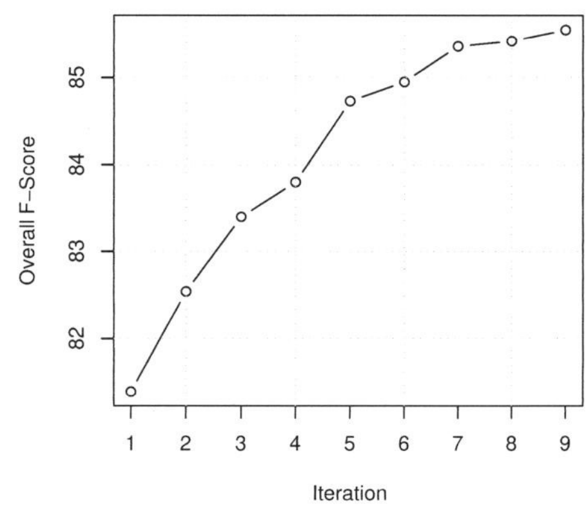

Figure 2: Overall F-score vs iteration numbers

Table 7 compares the results when the multi-mention property is also used in testing as a high-precision rule. Comparing Table 7 to Table 6, we can see that with the same training data, using multi-mention property helps improve classification results. However, this improvement is less than that obtained by using this property to extract training data thus improve the model itself. (For a fair comparison, the model used in the semi-supervised algorithm in Table 6 only uses multi-mention property to extract data.)

Our last experiment is to test how this method can be used when the initial gold data and the testing data are from different domains. We use the CoNLL 2003 English NER (Sang and Meulder, 2003) training set as the initial training data, and automatically extract training data from the TF financial news corpus. The CoNLL data is a collection of news wire documents from the Reuters Corpus, while TF data includes financial-related news only. Table 8 illustrates the results. As shown in the table, with only CoNLL data, although it contains around 220,000 tokens, the results are not better than the results when only 60 TF docs (Table 6) are used for training. This indicates that data from different domains can adversely affect NER accuracy for supervised learning. However, the semi-supervised algorithm achieves reasonably high accuracy. For LOC, ORG, and PER, the recall increases 16, 20.3, and 4.7 respectively, and the precision increases 4.5, 5.5, and 4.7 respectively. Therefore our semi-supervised approach is effective for situation where the test and training data are from different sources.

Table 7: Classification results when multi-mention property (M) is used in testing

Trainig Data	P/R(LOC)	P/R(ORG)	P/R(PER)
60 docs +M	89.9/87.6	82.4/71.4	78.2/87.3
700 docs+M	91.2/89.1 (1.3/1.5)	90.2/78.3 (7.8/6.9)	79.4/91.1 (1.2/3.8)
semi-supervised +M (60 docs)	90.0/91.0 (1.1/3.4)	86.6/82.4 (4.2/11.0)	81.3/90.6 (3.1/3.3)

Table 8: Classification results trained on CoNLL data and test on TF data. Training data for the semi-supervised algorithm are automatically extracted using both multi-mention and high-precision context from TF corpus.

Training Data	P/R(LOC)	P/R(ORG)	P/R(PER)
CoNLL	85.6/74.7	75.2/65.9	72.4/85.2
Semi-supervised (CoNLL)	90.1/90.7 **(4.5/16)**	81.7/86.2 **(5.5/20.3)**	77.1/90.5 **(4.7/4.7)**

6 Conclusion

We presented a simple semi-supervised learning algorithm for NER using conditional random fields (CRFs). In addition we proposed using high precision label features to improve classification accuracy as well as to reduce training and test time.

Compared to other semi-supervised learning algorithm, our proposed algorithm has several advantages. It is domain and data independent. Although it requires a small amount of labeled training data, the data is not required to be from the same domain as the one in which are interested to tag NEs. It can be applied to different types of NEs as long as independent evidence exists, which is usually available. It is simple and, we believe not limited by the choice of the classifier. Although we used CRFs in our framework, other models can be easily incorporated to our framework as long as they provide accurate confidence scores. With only a small amount of training data, our algorithm can achieve a better NE tagging accuracy than a supervised algorithm with a large amount of training data.

References

A. Blum and T. Mitchell. 1998. Combining labeled and unlabeled data with co-training. *Proceedings of the Workshop on Computational Learning Theory*, pages 92–100.

Michael Collins and Yoram Singer. 1999. Unsupervised models for named entity classification. *Proceedings of the Joint SIGDAT Conference on Empirical Methods in Natural Language Processing and Very Large Corpora.*

A. Culotta and A. McCallum. 2004. Confidence estimation for information extraction. *HLT-NAACL.*

G. D. Forney. 1973. The viterbi algorithm. *Proceedings of the IEEE*, 61(3):268–278.

Feng Jiao, Shaojun Wang, Chi H. Lee, Russell Greiner, and Dale Schuurmans. 2006. Semi-supervised conditional random fields for improved sequence segmentation and labeling. In *Proceedings of the 21st International Conference on Computational Linguistics*, pages 209–216, July.

Andrew McCallum and Wei Li. 2003. Early results for named entity recognition with conditional random fields, feature induction and web-enhanced lexicons. *CoNLL.*

A.K. McCallum. 2002. Mallet: A machine learning for language toolkit. http://mallet.cs.umass.edu.

Andrew McCallum. 2003. Efficiently inducing features of conditional random fields.

David Pierce and Claire Cardie. 2001. Limitations of co-training for natural language learning from large datasets. In *EMNLP.*

Erik F. Tjong Kim Sang and Fien De Meulder. 2003. Introduction to the conll-2003 shared task: Language-independent named entity recognition. *CoNLL*, pages 142–147.

Yingchuan Wong and Hwee Tou Ng. 2007. One class per named entity: Exploiting unlabeled text for named entity recognition. *IJCAI*, pages 1763–1768.

David Yarowsky. 1995. Unsupervised word sense disambiguation rivaling supervised methods. In *Meeting of the Association for Computational Linguistics*, pages 189–196.

Can One Language Bootstrap the Other: A Case Study on Event Extraction

Zheng Chen **Heng Ji**
Department of Computer Science
The Graduate Center Queens College and The Graduate Center
The City University of New York
365 Fifth Avenue, New York, NY 10016, USA
zchen1@gc.cuny.edu hengji@cs.qc.cuny.edu

Abstract

This paper proposes a new bootstrapping framework using cross-lingual information projection. We demonstrate that this framework is particularly effective for a challenging NLP task which is situated at the end of a pipeline and thus suffers from the errors propagated from upstream processing and has low-performance baseline. Using Chinese event extraction as a case study and bitexts as a new source of information, we present three bootstrapping techniques. We first conclude that the standard mono-lingual bootstrapping approach is not so effective. Then we exploit a second approach that potentially benefits from the extra information captured by an English event extraction system and projected into Chinese. Such a cross-lingual scheme produces significant performance gain. Finally we show that the combination of mono-lingual and cross-lingual information in bootstrapping can further enhance the performance. Ultimately this new framework obtained 10.1% relative improvement in trigger labeling (F-measure) and 9.5% relative improvement in argument-labeling.

1 Introduction

Bootstrapping methods can reduce the efforts needed to develop a training set and have shown promise in improving the performance of many tasks such as name tagging (Miller et al., 2004; Ji and Grishman, 2006), semantic class extraction (Lin et al., 2003), chunking (Ando and Zhang, 2005), coreference resolution (Bean and Riloff, 2004) and text classification (Blum and Mitchell, 1998). Most of these bootstrapping methods implicitly assume that:

- There exists a high-accuracy 'seed set' or 'seed model' as the baseline;
- There exists unlabeled data which is reliable and relevant to the test set in some aspects, e.g. from similar time frames and news sources; and therefore the unlabeled data supports the acquisition of new information, to provide new evidence to be incorporated to bootstrap the model and reduce the sparse data problem.
- The seeds and unlabeled data won't make the old estimates worse by adding too many incorrect instances.

However, for some more comprehensive and challenging tasks such as event extraction, the performance of the seed model suffers from the limited annotated training data and also from the errors propagated from upstream processing such as part-of-speech tagging and parsing. In addition, simply relying upon large unlabeled corpora cannot compensate for these limitations because more errors can be propagated from upstream processing such as entity extraction and temporal expression identification.

Inspired from the idea of co-training (Blum and Mitchell, 1998), in this paper we intend to bootstrap an event extraction system in one language (Chinese) by exploring new evidences from the event extraction system in another language (English) via cross-lingual projection. We conjecture that the *cross-lingual bootstrapping* for event extraction can naturally fit the co-training model: a same event is represented in two "views" (described in two languages). Furthermore, the cross-lingual bootstrapping can benefit from the different sources of training data. For example, the Chinese training corpus includes articles from Chinese new agencies in 2000 while most of English training data are from the US news agencies in 2003, thus English and Chinese event extraction systems have

Proceedings of the NAACL HLT Workshop on Semi-supervised Learning for Natural Language Processing, pages 66–74,
Boulder, Colorado, June 2009.

the nature of generating different results on parallel documents and may complement each other. In this paper, we explore approaches of exploiting the increasingly available bilingual parallel texts (***bitexts***).

We first investigate whether we can improve a Chinese event extraction system by simply using the Chinese side of bitexts in a regular monolingual bootstrapping framework. By gradually increasing the size of the corpus with unlabeled data, we did not get much improvement for trigger labeling and even observed performance deterioration for argument labeling. But then by aligning the texts at the word level, we found that the English event extraction results can be projected into Chinese for bootstrapping and lead to significant improvement. We also obtained clear further improvement by combining mono-lingual and cross-lingual bootstrapping.

The main contributions of this paper are two-fold. We formulate a new algorithm of cross-lingual bootstrapping, and demonstrate its effectiveness in a challenging task of event extraction; and we conclude that, for some applications besides machine translation, effective use of bitexts can be beneficial.

The remainder of the paper is organized as follows. Section 2 formalizes the event extraction task addressed in this paper. Section 3 discusses event extraction bootstrapping techniques. Section 4 reports our experimental results. Section 5 presents related work. Section 6 concludes this paper and points out future directions.

2 Event Extraction

2.1 Task Definition and Terminology

The event extraction that we address in this paper is specified in the Automatic Content Extraction (ACE)[1] program. The ACE 2005 Evaluation defines the following terminology for the event extraction task:

- **event trigger**: the word that most clearly expresses an event's occurrence
- **event argument**: an *entity*, a *temporal expression* or a *value* that plays a certain *role* in the event instance
- **event mention**: a phrase or sentence with a distinguished trigger and participant arguments

[1] http://www.nist.gov/speech/tests/ace/

The event extraction task in our paper is to detect certain types of event mentions that are indicated by event triggers (*trigger labeling*), recognize the event participants e.g., *who, when, where, how* (*argument labeling*) and merge the co-referenced event mentions into a unified event (*post-processing*). In this paper, we focus on discussing trigger labeling and argument labeling.

In the following example,

Mike got married in 2008.

The event extraction system should identify "*married*" as the event trigger which indicates the event type of "Life" and subtype of "Marry". Furthermore, it should detect "*Mike*" and "*2008*" as arguments in which "*Mike*" has a role of "Person" and "*2008*" has a role of "Time-Within".

2.2 A Pipeline of Event Extraction

Our pipeline framework of event extraction includes trigger labeling, argument labeling and post-processing, similar to (Grishman et al., 2005), (Ahn, 2006) and (Chen and Ji, 2009). We depict the framework as Figure 1.

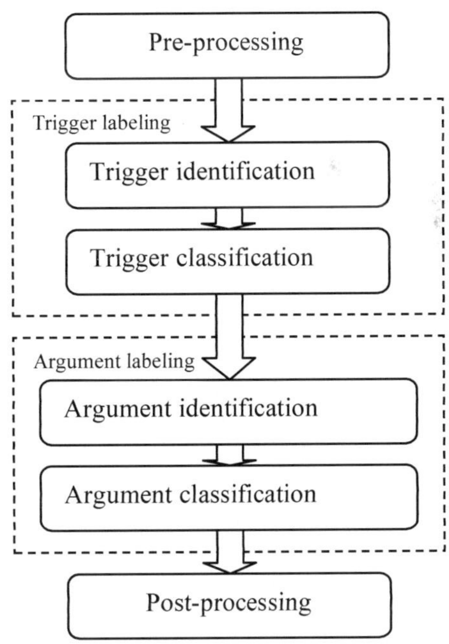

Figure 1. Pipeline of Event Extraction

The event extraction system takes raw documents as input and conducts some pre-processing steps. The texts are automatically annotated with word segmentation, Part-of-Speech tags, parsing structures, entities, time expressions, and relations.

The annotated documents are then sent to the following four components. Each component is a classifier and produces confidence values;

- Trigger identification: the classifier recognizes a word or a phrase as the event trigger.
- Trigger classification: the classifier assigns an event type to an identified trigger.
- Argument identification: the classifier recognizes whether an entity, temporal expression or value is an argument associated with a particular trigger in the same sentence.
- Argument classification: the classifier assigns a role to the argument.

The post-processing merges co-referenced event mentions into a unified representation of event.

2.3 Two Monolingual Event Extraction Systems

We use two monolingual event extraction systems, one for English, and the other for Chinese. Both systems employ the above framework and use Maximum Entropy based classifiers. The corresponding classifiers in both systems also share some language-independent features, for example, in trigger identification, both classifiers use the "previous word" and "next word" as features, however, there are some language-dependent features that only work well for one monolingual system, for example, in argument identification, the next word of the candidate argument is a good feature for Chinese system but not for English system. To illustrate this, in the Chinese "*的*" (*of*) structure, the word "*的*" (*of*) strongly suggests that the entity on the left side of "*的*" is not an argument. For a specific example, in "*纽约市的市长*" (*The mayor of New York City*), "*纽约市*" (*New York City*) on the left side of "*的*" (*of*) cannot be considered as an argument because it is a modifier of the noun "*市长*"(*mayor*). Unlike Chinese, "*of*" ("*的*") appears ahead of the entity in the English phrase.

Table 1 lists the overall Precision (P), Recall (R) and F-Measure (F) scores for trigger labeling and argument labeling in our two monolingual event extraction systems. For comparison, we also list the performance of an English human annotator and a Chinese human annotator.

Table 1 shows that event extraction is a difficult NLP task because even human annotators cannot achieve satisfying performance. Both monolingual systems relied on expensive human labeled data (much more expensive than other NLP tasks due to the extra tagging tasks of entities and temporal expressions), thus a natural question arises: can the monolingual system benefit from bootstrapping techniques with a relative small set of training data? The other question is: can a monolingual system benefit from the other monolingual system by cross-lingual bootstrapping?

Performance / System/Human	Trigger Labeling			Argument Labeling		
	P	R	F	P	R	F
English System	64.3	59.4	61.8	49.2	34.7	40.7
Chinese System	78.8	48.3	59.9	60.6	34.3	43.8
English Annotator	59.2	59.4	59.3	51.6	59.5	55.3
Chinese Annotator	75.2	74.6	74.9	58.6	60.9	59.7

Table 1.Performance of Two Monolingual Event Extraction Systems and Human Annotators

3 Bootstrapping Event Extraction

3.1 General Bootstrapping Algorithm

Bootstrapping algorithms have attracted much attention from researchers because a large number of unlabeled examples are available and can be utilized to boost the performance of a system trained on a small set of labeled examples. The general bootstrapping algorithm is depicted in Figure 2, similar to (Mihalcea, 2004).

Self-training and Co-training are two most commonly used bootstrapping methods.

A typical self-training process is described as follows: it starts with a set of training examples and builds a classifier with the full integrated feature set. The classifier is then used to label an additional portion of the unlabeled examples. Among the resulting labeled examples, put the most confident ones into the training set, and re-train the classifier. This iterates until a certain condition is satisfied (e.g., all the unlabeled examples have been labeled, or it reaches a certain number of iterations).

Co-training(Blum and Mitchell, 1998) differs from self-training in that it assumes that the data can be represented using two or more separate "views" (thus the whole feature set is split into disjoint feature subsets) and each classifier can be trained on one view of the data. For each iteration, both classifiers label an additional portion of the unlabeled examples and put the most confident ones to the training set. Then the two classifiers are retrained on the new training set and iterate until a certain condition is satisfied.

Both self-training and co-training can fit in the general bootstrapping process. If the number of classifiers is set to one, it is a self-training process, and it is a co-training process if there are two different classifiers that interact in the bootstrapping process.

Input:
  L : a set of labeled examples,
  U : a set of unlabeled examples
  $\{C_i\}$: a set of classifiers
Initialization:
  Create a pool U¢of examples by choosing P random examples from U
Loop until a condition is satisfied (e.g., U =Æ , or iteration counter reaches a preset number I)
- Train each classifier C_i on L, and label the examples in U¢
- For each classifier C_i ,select the most confidently labeled examples (e.g., the confidence score is above a preset threshold $q$or the top K) and add them to L
- Refill U¢with examples from U , and keep the size of U¢ as constant P

Figure 2. General Bootstrapping Algorithm.

In the following sections, we adapt the bootstrapping techniques discussed in this section to a larger scale (system level). In other words, we aim to bootstrap the overall performance of the system which may include multiple classifiers, rather than just improve the performance of a single classifier in the system. It is worth noting that for the pipeline event extraction depicted in Section 2.2, there are two major steps that determine the overall system performance: trigger labeling and argument labeling. Furthermore, the performance of trigger labeling can directly affect the performance of argument labeling because the involving arguments are constructed according to the trigger. If a trigger is wrongly recognized, all the involving arguments will be considered as wrong arguments. If a trigger is missing, all the attached arguments will be considered as missing arguments.

3.2 Monolingual Self-training

It is rather smooth to adapt the idea of traditional self-training to monolingual self-training if we consider our monolingual event extraction system as a black box or even a single classifier that determines whether an event combining the result of trigger labeling and argument labeling is a reportable event.

Thus the monolingual self-training procedure for event extraction is quite similar with the one described in Section 3.1. The monolingual event extraction system is first trained on a starting set of labeled documents, and then tag on an additional portion of unlabeled documents. Note that in each labeled document, multiple events could be tagged and confidence score is assigned to each event. Then the labeled documents are added into the training set and the system is retrained based on the events with high confidence. This iterates until all the unlabeled documents have been tagged.

3.3 Cross-lingual Co-Training

We extend the idea of co-training to cross-lingual co-training. The intuition behind cross-lingual co-training is that the same event has different "views" described in different languages, because the lexical unit, the grammar and sentence construction differ from one language to the other. Thus one monolingual event extraction system probably utilizes the language dependent features that cannot work well for the other monolingual event extraction systems. Blum and Mitchell (1998) derived PAC-like guarantees on learning under two assumptions: 1) the two views are individually sufficient for classification and 2) the two views are conditionally independent given the class. Obviously, the first assumption can be satisfied in cross-lingual co-training for event extraction, since each monolingual event extraction system is sufficient for event extraction task. However, we reserve our opinion on the second assumption. Although the two monolingual event extraction systems may apply the same language-independent features such as the part-of-speech, the next word and the previous word, the features are exhibited in their own context of language, thus it is too subjective to conclude that the two feature sets are or are not conditionally independent. It is left to be an unsolved issue which needs further strict analysis and supporting experiments.

The cross-lingual co-training differs from traditional co-training in that the two systems in cross-lingual co-training are not initially trained from the same labeled data. Furthermore, in the bootstrapping phase, each system only labels half portion of the bitexts in its own language. In order to utilize the labeling result by the other system, we need to conduct an extra step named *cross-lingual projection* that transforms tagged events from one language to the other.

3.3.1 A Cross-lingual Co-training Algorithm

The algorithm for cross-lingual co-training is depicted in Figure 3.

Input:

L_1: a set of labeled examples in language A

L_2: a set of labeled examples in language B

U : a set of unlabeled bilingual examples (bitexts) with alignment information

$\{S_1, S_2\}$: two monolingual systems, one for language A and the other for language B.

Initialization:

Create a pool U' of examples by choosing P random examples from U

Loop until a condition is satisfied (e.g., $U = \emptyset$, or iteration counter reaches a preset number I)

- Train S_1 on L_1 and S_2 on L_2
- Use S_1 to label the examples in U' (the portion in Language A) and use S_2 to label the examples in U' (the portion in Language B)
- For S_1, select the most confidently labeled examples (e.g., the confidence score is above a preset threshold θ or the top K), apply the operation of cross-lingual projection, transform the selected examples from Language A to Language B, and put them into L_2. The same procedure applies to S_2.
- Refill U' with examples from U , and keep the size of U' as constant P

Figure 3. Cross-lingual Co-training Algorithm

3.3.2 Cross-lingual Semi-co-training

Cross-lingual semi-co-training is a variation of cross-lingual co-training, and it differs from cross-lingual co-training in that it tries to bootstrap only one system by the other fine-trained system. This technique is helpful when we have relatively large amount of training data in one language while we have scarce data in the other language.

Thus we only need to make a small modification in the cross-lingual co-training algorithm so that it can soon be adapted to cross-lingual semi-co-training, i.e., we retrain one system and do not retrain the other. In this paper, we will conduct experiments to investigate whether a fine-trained English event extraction system can bootstrap the Chinese event extraction system, starting from a small set of training data.

3.3.3 Cross-lingual Projection

Cross-lingual projection is a key operation in the cross-lingual co-training algorithm. In the case of event extraction, we need to project the triggers and the participant arguments from one language into the other language according to the alignment information provided by bitexts. Figure 4 shows an example of projecting an English event into the corresponding Chinese event.

Before projection:

```
<event ID="chtb_282-EV1" TYPE="Contact" SUBTYPE="Meet">
  <event_mention ID="chtb_282-EV1-1" p="1.000">
    <trigger>
      <charseq START="2259" END="2265">meeting</charseq>
    </ trigger >
    <event_mention_argument ROLE="Entity" p="0.704" pRole="0.924"/>
      <extent>
        <charseq START="2238" END="2244">Gan Luo</charseq>
      </extent>
    </event_mention_argument>
  </event_mention>
</event>
```

After projection:

```
<event ID="chtb_282-EV1" TYPE="Contact" SUBTYPE="Meet">
  <event_mention ID="chtb_282-EV1-1" p="1.000">
    <trigger>
      <charseq START="454" END="455">会见</charseq>
    </ trigger >
    <event_mention_argument ROLE="Entity" p="0.704" pRole="0.924"/>
      <extent>
        <charseq START="449" END="450">罗干</charseq>
      </extent>
    </event_mention_argument>
  </event_mention>
</event>
```

Figure 4. An Example of Cross-lingual Projection

4 Experiments and Results

4.1 Data and Scoring Metric

We used the ACE 2005 corpus to set up two monolingual event extraction systems, one for English, the other for Chinese.

The ACE 2005 corpus contains 560 English documents from 6 sources: newswire, broadcast news, broadcast conversations, weblogs, newsgroups and conversational telephone speech; meanwhile the corpus contains 633 Chinese documents from 3 sources: newswire, broadcast news and weblogs.

We then use 159 texts from the LDC Chinese Treebank English Parallel corpus with manual alignment for our cross-lingual bootstrapping experiments.

We define the following standards to determine the *correctness* of an event mention:

- *A trigger is correctly labeled* if its event type and offsets match a reference trigger.
- *An argument is correctly labeled* if its event type, offsets, and role match any of the reference argument mentions.

4.2 Monolingual Self-training on ACE 2005 Data

We first investigate whether our Chinese event extraction system can benefit from monolingual self-training on ACE data. We reserve 66 Chinese documents for testing purpose and set the size of seed training set to 100. For a single trial of the experiment, we *randomly* select 100 documents as training set and use the remaining documents as self-training data. For each iteration of the self-training, we keep the pool size as 50, in other words, we always pick another 50 ACE documents to self-train the system. The iteration continues until all the unlabeled ACE documents have been tagged and thus it completes one trial of the experiment. We conduct the same experiment for 100 trials and compute the average scores.

The most important motivation for us to conduct self-training experiments on ACE data is that the ACE data provide ground-truth entities and temporal expressions so that we do not have to take into account the effects of propagated errors from upstream processing such as entity extraction and temporal expression identification.

For one setting of the experiments, we set the confidence threshold to 0, in other words, we keep all the labeling results for retraining. The results are given in Figure 5 (trigger labeling) and Figure 6 (argument labeling). It shows that when the number of self-trained ACE documents reaches 450, we obtain a gain of 3.4% (F-Measure) above the baseline for trigger labeling and a gain of 1.4% for argument labeling.

For the other setting of the experiments, we set the confidence threshold to 0.8, and the results are presented in Figure 7 and Figure 8. Surprisingly, retraining on the high confidence examples does not lead to much improvement. We obtain a gain of 3.7% above the baseline for trigger labeling and 1.5% for argument labeling when the number of self-trained documents reaches 450.

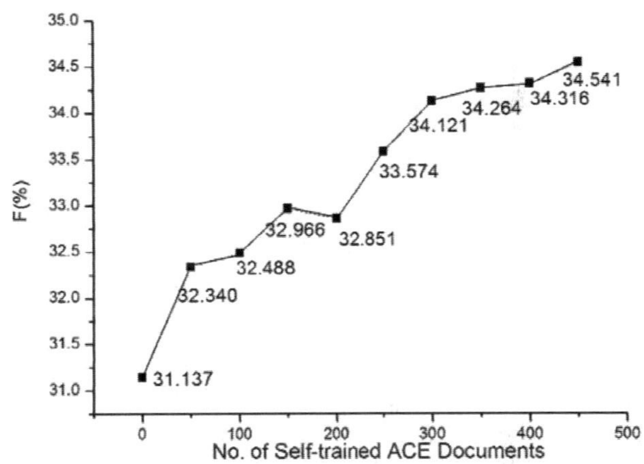

Figure 5. Self-training for trigger labeling (confidence threshold = 0)

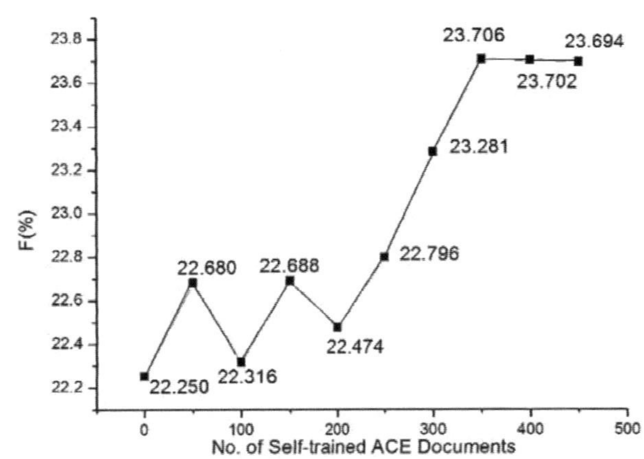

Figure 6. Self-training for argument labeling (confidence threshold= 0)

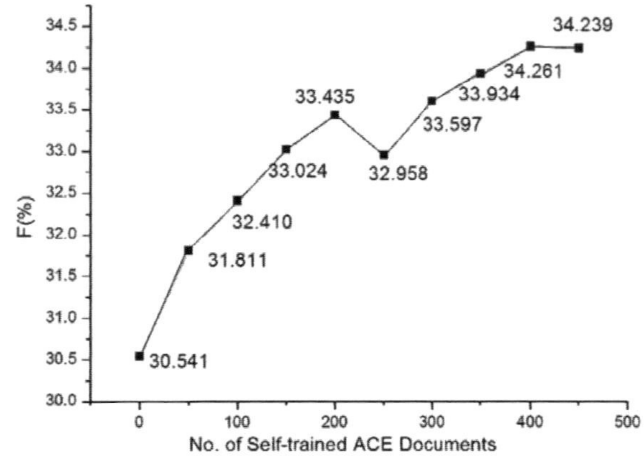

Figure 7. Self-training for trigger labeling (confidence threshold = 0.8)

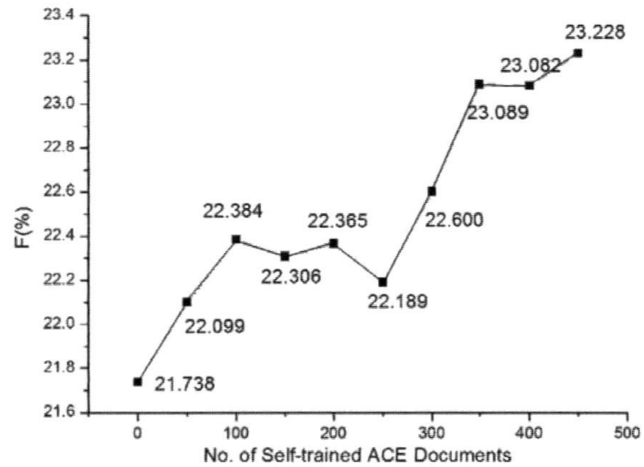

Figure 8. Self-training for argument labeling (confidence threshold = 0.8)

4.3 Cross-lingual Semi-co-training on Bitexts

The experiments in Section 4.2 show that we can obtain gain in performance by monolingual self-training on data with ground-truth entities and temporal expressions, but what if we do not have such ground-truth data, then how the errors propagated from entity extraction and temporal expression identification will affect the overall performance of our event extraction system? And if these errors are compounded in event extraction, can the cross-lingual semi-co-training alleviate the impact?

To investigate all these issues, we use 159 texts from LDC Chinese Treebank English Parallel corpus to conduct cross-lingual semi-co-training. The experimental results are summarized in Figure 9 and Figure 10.

For monolingual self-training on the bitexts, we conduct experiments exactly as section 4.2 except that the entities are tagged by the IE system and the labeling pool size is set to 20. When the number of bitexts reaches 159, we obtain a little gain of 0.4% above the baseline for trigger labeling and a loss of 0.1% below the baseline for argument labeling. The deterioration tendency of the self-training curve in Figure 10 indicates that entity extraction errors do have counteractive impacts on argument labeling.

We then conduct the cross-lingual semi-co-training experiments as follows: we set up an English event extraction system trained on a relative large training set (500 documents). For each trial of the experiment, we randomly select 100 ACE Chinese document as seed training set, and then it enters a cross-lingual semi-co-training process: for each iteration, the English system labels the English portions of the 20 bitexts and by cross-lingual projection, the labeled results are transformed into Chinese and put into the training set of Chinese system. From Figure 9 and Figure 10 we can see that when the number of bitexts reaches 159, we obtain a gain of 1.7% for trigger labeling and 0.7% for argument labeling.

We then apply a third approach to bootstrap our Chinese system: during each iteration, the Chinese system also labels the Chinese portions of the 20 bitexts. Then we combine the results from both monolingual systems using the following rules:

- If the event labeled by English system is not labeled by Chinese system, add the event to Chinese system
- If the event labeled by Chinese system is not labeled by English system, keep the event in the Chinese system
- If both systems label the same event but with different event types and arguments, select the one with higher confidence

From Figure 9 and Figure 10 we can see that this approach leads to even further improvement in performance, shown as the "Combined-labeled" curves. When the number of bitexts reaches 159, we obtain a gain of 3.1% for trigger labeling and 2.1% for argument labeling.

In order to check how robust our approach is, we conducted the Wilcoxon Matched-Pairs Signed-Ranks Test on F-measures for all these 100 trials. The results show that we can reject the hypotheses that the improvements using Cross-lingual Semi-co-training were random at a 99.99% confidence level, for both trigger labeling and argument labeling.

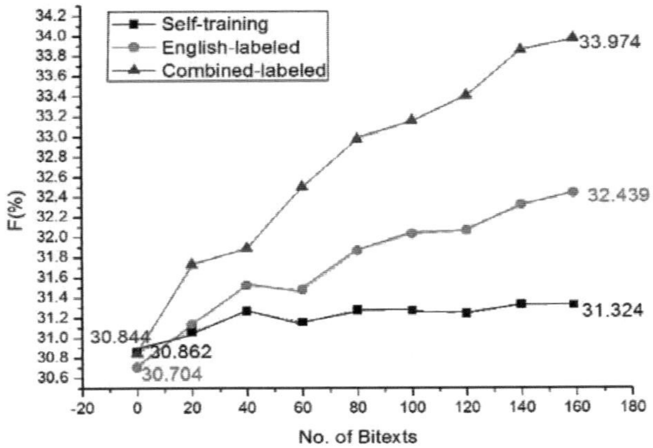

Figure 9. Self-training, and Semi-co-training (English- labeled & Combined-labeled) for Trigger Labeling

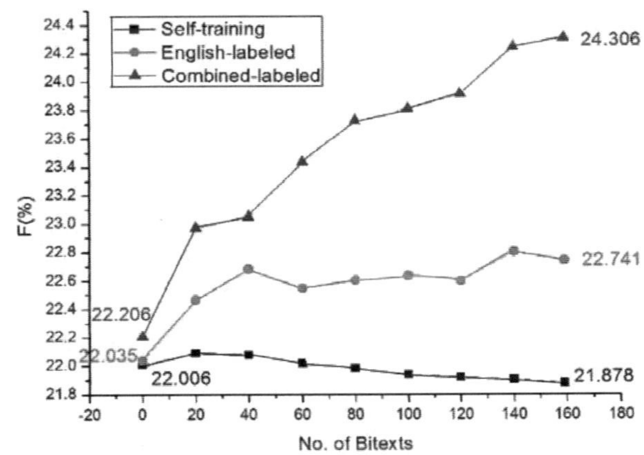

Figure 10. Self-training, and Semi-co-training (English- labeled & Combined-labeled) for Argument Labeling

5 Related Work

There is a huge literature on utilizing parallel corpus for monolingual improvement. To our knowledge, it can retrace to (Dagan et.al 1991). We apologize to those whose work is not cited due to space constraints. The work described here complements some recent research using bitexts or translation techniques as feedback to improve entity extraction. Huang and Vogel (2002) presented an effective integrated approach that can improve the extracted named entity translation dictionary and the entity annotation in a bilingual training corpus. Ji and Grishman (2007) expanded this idea of alignment consistency to the task of entity extraction in a monolingual test corpus without reference translations, and applied sophisticated inference rules to enhance both entity extraction and translation. Zitouni and Florian (2008) applied English mention detection on translated texts and added the results as additional features to improve mention detection in other languages.

In this paper we share the similar idea of importing evidences from English with richer resources to improve extraction in other languages. However, to the best of our knowledge this is the first work of incorporating cross-lingual feedback to improve the event extraction task. More importantly, it is the first attempt of combining cross-lingual projection with bootstrapping methods, which can avoid the efforts of designing sophisticated inference rules or features.

6 Conclusions and Future Work

Event extraction remains a difficult task not only because it is situated at the end of an IE pipeline and thus suffers from the errors propagated from upstream processing, but also because the labeled data are expensive and thus suffers from data scarcity. In this paper, we proposed a new co-training framework using cross-lingual information projection and demonstrate that the additional information from English system can be used to bootstrap a Chinese event extraction system.

To move a step forward, we would like to conduct experiments on cross-lingual co-training and investigate whether the two systems on both sides can benefit from each other. A main issue existing in cross-lingual co-training is that the cross-lingual projection may not be perfect due to the word alignment problem. In this paper, we used a corpus with manual alignment, but in the future we intend to investigate the effect of automatic alignment errors.

We believe that the proposed cross-lingual bootstrapping framework can also be applied to many other challenging NLP tasks such as relation extraction. However, we still need to provide a theoretical analysis of the framework.

Acknowledgments

This material is based upon work supported by the Defense Advanced Research Projects Agency under Contract No. HR0011-06-C-0023 via 27-001022, and the CUNY Research Enhancement Program and GRTI Program.

References

Avrim Blum and Tom Mitchell. 1998. Combining Labeled and Unlabeled Data with Co-training. *Proc. of the Workshop on Computational Learning Theory*. Morgan Kaufmann Publishers.

David Ahn. 2006. The stages of event extraction. Proc. COLING/ACL 2006 Workshop on Annotating and Reasoning about Time and Events. Sydney, Australia.

David Bean and Ellen Riloff. 2004. Unsupervised Learning of Contextual Role Knowledge for Coreference Resolution. *Proc. HLT-NAACL2004*. pp. 297-304. Boston, USA.

Fei Huang and Stephan Vogel. 2002. Improved Named Entity Translation and Bilingual Named Entity Extraction. *Proc. ICMI 2002*. Pittsburgh, PA, US.

Heng Ji and Ralph Grishman. 2006. Data Selection in Semi-supervised Learning for Name Tagging. *In ACL 2006 Workshop on Information Extraction Beyond the Document:48-55*. Sydney, Australia.

Heng Ji and Ralph Grishman. 2007. Collaborative Entity Extraction and Translation. *Proc. International Conference on Recent Advances in Natural Language Processing 2007*. Borovets, Bulgaria.

Ido Dagan, Alon Itai and Ulrike Schwall. 1991. Two languages are more informative than one. *Proc. ACL 1991*.

Imed Zitouni and Radu Florian. 2008. Mention Detection Crossing the Language Barrier. *Proc. EMNLP*. Honolulu, Hawaii.

Michael Collins and Yoram Singer. 1999. Unsupervised Models for Named Entity Classification. *Proc. of EMNLP/VLC-99*.

Rada Mihalcea. 2004. Co-training and self-training for word sense disambiguation. In Proceedings of the Conference on Computational Natural Language Learning (CoNLL-2004).

Ralph Grishman, David Westbrook and Adam Meyers. 2005. NYU's English ACE 2005 System Description. *Proc. ACE 2005 Evaluation Workshop*. Washington, US.

Rie Ando and Tong Zhang. 2005. A High-Performance Semi-Supervised Learning Methods for Text Chunking. *Proc. ACL2005*. pp. 1-8. Ann Arbor, USA

Scott Miller, Jethran Guinness and Alex Zamanian.2004. Name Tagging with Word Clusters and Discriminative Training. *Proc. HLT-NAACL2004*. pp. 337-342. Boston, USA

Winston Lin, Roman Yangarber and Ralph Grishman. 2003. Bootstrapping Learning of Semantic Classes from Positive and Negative Examples. *Proc. ICML-2003 Workshop on The Continuum from Labeled to Unlabeled Data*. Washington, D.C.

Zheng Chen and Heng Ji. 2009. Language Specific Issue and Feature Exploration in Chinese Event Extraction. *Proc. HLT-NAACL 2009*. Boulder, Co.

On Semi-Supervised Learning of Gaussian Mixture Models for Phonetic Classification*

Jui-Ting Huang and Mark Hasegawa-Johnson
Department of Electrical and Computer Engineering
University of Illinois at Urbana-Champaign
Illinois, IL 61801, USA
{jhuang29,jhasegaw}@illinois.edu

Abstract

This paper investigates semi-supervised learning of Gaussian mixture models using an unified objective function taking both labeled and unlabeled data into account. Two methods are compared in this work – the hybrid discriminative/generative method and the purely generative method. They differ in the criterion type on labeled data; the hybrid method uses the class posterior probabilities and the purely generative method uses the data likelihood. We conducted experiments on the TIMIT database and a standard synthetic data set from UCI Machine Learning repository. The results show that the two methods behave similarly in various conditions. For both methods, unlabeled data improve training on models of higher complexity in which the supervised method performs poorly. In addition, there is a trend that more unlabeled data results in more improvement in classification accuracy over the supervised model. We also provided experimental observations on the relative weights of labeled and unlabeled parts of the training objective and suggested a critical value which could be useful for selecting a good weighing factor.

1 Introduction

Speech recognition acoustic models can be trained using untranscribed speech data (Wessel and Ney, 2005; Lamel et al., 2002; L. Wang and Woodland, 2007). Most such experiments begin by boostraping an initial acoustic model using a limited amount of manually transcribed data (normally in a scale from 30 minutes to several hours), and then the initial model is used to transcribe a relatively large amount of untranscribed data. Only the transcriptions with high confidence measures (Wessel and Ney, 2005; L. Wang and Woodland, 2007) or high agreement with closed captions (Lamel et al., 2002) are selected to augment the manually transcribed data, and new acoustic models are trained on the augmented data set.

The general procedure described above exactly lies in the context of semi-supervised learning problems and can be categorized as a self-training algorithm. Self-training is probably the simplest semi-supervised learning method, but it is also flexible to be applied to complex classifiers such as speech recognition systems. This may be the reason why little work has been done on exploiting other semi-supervised learning methods in speech recognition. Though not incorporated to speech recognizers yet, there has been some work on semi-supervised learning of Hidden Markov Models (HMM) for sequential classification. Inoue and Ueda (2003) treated the unknown class labels of the unlabeled data as hidden variables and used the expectation-maximization (EM) algorithm to optimize the joint likelihood of labeled and unlabeled data. Recently Ji et al. (2009) applied a homotopy method to select the optimal weight to balance between the log likelihood of labeled and unlabeled data when training HMMs.

Besides generative training of acoustic models, discriminative training is another popular paradigm in the area of speech recognition, but only when

*This research is funded by NSF grants 0534106 and 0703624.

Proceedings of the NAACL HLT Workshop on Semi-supervised Learning for Natural Language Processing, pages 75–83,
Boulder, Colorado, June 2009.

the transcriptions are available. Wang and Woodland (2007) used the self-training method to augment the training set for discriminative training. Huang and Hasegawa-Johnson (2008) investigated another use of discriminative information from labeled data by replacing the likelihood of labeled data with the class posterior probability of labeled data in the semi-supervised training objective for Gaussian Mixture Models (GMM), resulting in a hybrid discriminative/generative objective function. Their experimental results in binary phonetic classification showed significant improvement in classification accuracy when labeled data are scarce. A similar strategy called "'multi-conditional learning"' was presented in (Druck et al., 2007) applied to Markov Random Field models for text classification tasks, with the difference that the likelihood of labeled data is also included in the objective. The hybrid discriminative/generative objective function can be interpreted as having an extra regularization term, the likelihood of unlabeled data, in the discriminative training criterion for labeled data. However, both methods in (Huang and Hasegawa-Johnson, 2008) and (Druck et al., 2007) encountered the same issue about determining the weights for labeled and unlabeled part in the objective function and chose to use a development set to select the optimal weight. This paper provides an experimental analysis on the effect of the weight.

With the ultimate goal of applying semi-supervised learning in speech recognition, this paper investigates the learning capability of algorithms within Gaussian Mixture Models because GMM is the basic model inside a HMM, therefore 1) the update equations derived for the parameters of GMM can be conveniently extended to HMM for speech recognition. 2) GMM can serve as an initial point to help us understand more details about the semi-supervised learning process of spectral features.

This paper makes the following contribution:

- it provides an experimental comparison of hybrid and purely generative training objectives.
- it studies the impact of model complexity on learning capability of algorithms.
- it studies the impact of the amount of unlabeled data on learning capability of algorithms.
- it analyzes the role of the relative weights of labeled and unlabeled parts of the training objective.

2 Algorithm

Suppose a labeled set $\mathcal{X}_L = (x_1, \ldots, x_n, \ldots, x_{N_L})$ has N_L data points and $x_n \in \mathcal{R}_d$. $\mathcal{Y}_L = (y_1, \ldots, y_n, \ldots, y_{N_L})$ are the corresponding class labels, where $y_n \in \{1, 2, \ldots, Y\}$ and Y is the number of classes. In addition, we also have an unlabeled set $\mathcal{X}_U = (x_1, \ldots, x_n, \ldots, x_{N_U})$ without corresponding class labels. Each class is assigned a Gaussian Mixture model, and all models are trained given $\mathcal{X}_L$ and $\mathcal{X}_U$. This section first presents the hybrid discriminative/generative objective function for training and then the purely generative objective function. The parameter update equations are also derived here.

2.1 Hybrid Objective Function

The hybrid discriminative/generative objective function combines the discriminative criterion for labeled data and the generative criterion for unlabeled data:

$$\mathcal{F}(\lambda) = \log P(\mathcal{Y}_L|\mathcal{X}_L; \lambda) + \alpha \log P(\mathcal{X}_U; \lambda), \quad (1)$$

and we chose the parameters so that (1) is maximized:

$$\hat{\lambda} = \arg\max_{\lambda} \mathcal{F}(\lambda). \quad (2)$$

The first component considers the log posterior class probability of the labeled set whereas the second component considers the log likelihood of the unlabeled set weighted by α. In ASR community, model training based the first component is usually referred to as Maximum Mutual Information Estimation (MMIE) and the second component Maximum Likelihood Estimation (MLE), therefore in this paper we use a brief notation for (1) just for convenience:

$$\mathcal{F}(\lambda) = \mathcal{F}_{\text{MMI}}^{(D_L)}(\lambda) + \alpha \mathcal{F}_{\text{ML}}^{(D_U)}(\lambda). \quad (3)$$

The two components are different in scale. First, the size of the labeled set is usually smaller than the size of the unlabeled set in the scenario of semi-supervised learning, so the sums over the data sets involve different numbers of terms; Second, the scales of the posterior probability and the likelihood are essentially different, so are their gradients. While the weight α balances the impacts of two components on the training process, it may also implicitly normalize the scales of the two components. In section (3.2) we will discuss and provide a further experimental analysis.

In this paper, the models to be trained are Gaussian mixture models of continuous spectral feature vectors for phonetic classes, which can be further extended to Hidden Markov Models with extra parameters such as transition probabilities.

The maximization of (1) follows the techniques in (Povey, 2003), which uses auxiliary functions for objective maximization; In each iteration, a strong or weak sense auxiliary function is maximized, such that if the auxiliary function converges after iterations, the objective function will be at a local maximum as well.

The objective function (1) can be rewritten as

$$\mathcal{F}(\lambda) = \log P(\mathcal{X}_L|\mathcal{Y}_L;\lambda) - \log P(\mathcal{X}_L;\lambda) + \alpha \log P(\mathcal{X}_U;\lambda), \tag{4}$$

where the term $\log P(\mathcal{Y}_L;\lambda)$ is removed because it is independent of acoustic model parameters.

The auxiliary function at the current parameter λ^{old} for (4) is

$$\mathcal{G}(\lambda, \lambda^{(\text{old})}) = \mathcal{G}^{\text{num}}(\lambda, \lambda^{(\text{old})}) - \mathcal{G}^{\text{den}}(\lambda, \lambda^{(\text{old})}) + \alpha \mathcal{G}^{\text{den}}(\lambda, \lambda^{(\text{old})}; \mathcal{D}_U) + \mathcal{G}^{\text{sm}}(\lambda, \lambda^{(\text{old})}), \tag{5}$$

where the first three terms are strong-sense auxiliary functions for the conditional likelihood (referred to as the numerator(num) model because it appears in the numerator when computing the class posterior probability) $\log P(\mathcal{X}_L|\mathcal{Y}_L;\lambda)$ and the marginal likelihoods (referred to as the denominator(den) model likewise) $\log P(\mathcal{X}_L;\lambda)$ and $\alpha \log P(\mathcal{X}_U;\lambda)$ respectively. The last term is a smoothing function that doesn't affect the local differential but ensures that the sum of the first three term is at least a convex weak-sense auxiliary function for good convergence in optimization.

Maximization of (5) leads to the update equations for the class j and mixture m given as follows:

$$\hat{\mu}_{jm} = \frac{1}{\overline{\gamma}_{jm}} \left(\boldsymbol{x}_{jm,}^{\text{num}} - \boldsymbol{x}_{jm}^{\text{den}} + \alpha \boldsymbol{x}_{jm}^{\text{den}}(\mathcal{D}_U) + D_{jm}\mu_{jm} \right) \tag{6}$$

$$\hat{\sigma}_{jm}^2 = \frac{1}{\overline{\gamma}_{jm}} \left(\boldsymbol{s}_{jm}^{\text{num}} - \boldsymbol{s}_{jm}^{\text{den}} + \alpha \boldsymbol{s}_{jm}^{\text{den}}(\mathcal{D}_U) + D_{jm}\left(\sigma_{jm}^2 + \mu_{jm}^2\right)\right) - \hat{\mu}_{jm}^2, \tag{7}$$

where for clarity the following substitution is used:

$$\overline{\gamma}_{jm} = \gamma_{jm}^{\text{num}} - \gamma_{jm}^{\text{den}} + \alpha \gamma_{jm}^{\text{den}}(\mathcal{D}_U) + D_{jm} \tag{8}$$

and γ_{jm} is the sum of the posterior probabilities of occupation of mixture component m of class j over the dataset:

$$\gamma_{jm}^{\text{num}}(X) = \sum_{x_i \in X, y_i = j} p(m|x_i, y_i = j)$$
$$\gamma_{jm}^{\text{den}}(X) = \sum_{x_i \in X} p(m|x_i) \tag{9}$$

and $\boldsymbol{x}_{jm}$ and $\boldsymbol{s}_{jm}$ are respectively the weighted sum of x_i and x_i^2 over the whole dataset with the weight $p(m|x_i, y_i = j)$ or $p(m|x_i)$, depending on whether the superscript is the numerator or denominator model. D_{jm} is a constant set to be the greater of twice the smallest value that guarantees positive variances or γ_{jm}^{den} (Povey, 2003). The re-estimation formula for mixture weights is also derived from the Extended Baum-Welch algorithm:

$$\hat{c}_{jm} = \frac{c_{jm}\left\{\frac{\partial \mathcal{F}}{\partial c_{jm}} + C\right\}}{\sum_{m'} c_{jm'}\left\{\frac{\partial \mathcal{F}}{\partial c_{jm}} + C\right\}}, \tag{10}$$

where the derivative was approximated (Merialdo, 1988) in the following form for practical robustness for small-valued parameters :

$$\frac{\partial \mathcal{F}_{\text{MMI}}}{\partial c_{jm}} \approx \frac{\gamma_{jm}^{\text{num}}}{\sum_{m'} \gamma_{jm'}^{\text{num}}} - \frac{\gamma_{jm}^{\text{den}}}{\sum_{m'} \gamma_{jm'}^{\text{den}}}. \tag{11}$$

Under our hybrid framework, there is an extra term $\gamma_{jm}^{\text{den}}(D_U)/\sum_{m'} \gamma_{jm'}^{\text{den}}(D_U)$ that should exist in (11), but in practice we found that adding this term to the approximation is not better than the original form. Therefore, we keep using MMI-only update for mixture weights. The constant C is chosen such that all parameter derivatives are positive.

2.2 Purely Generative Objective

In this paper we compare the hybrid objective with the purely generative one:

$$\mathcal{F}(\lambda) = \log P(\mathcal{X}_L|\mathcal{Y}_L;\lambda) + \alpha \log P(\mathcal{X}_U;\lambda), \quad (12)$$

where the two components are total log likelihood of labeled and unlabeled data respectively. (12) doesn't suffer from the problem of combining two heterogeneous probabilistic items, and the weight α being equal to one means that the objective is a joint data likelihood of labeled and unlabeled set with the assumption that the two sets are independent. However, D_L or D_U might just be a sampled set of the population and might not reflect the true proportion, so we keep α to allow a flexible combination of two criteria. On top of that, we need to adjust the relative weights of the two components in practical experiments.

The parameter update equation is a reduced form of the equations in Section (2.1):

$$\hat{\mu}_{jm} = \frac{\boldsymbol{x}_{jm,}^{\text{num}} + \alpha \boldsymbol{x}_{jm}^{\text{den}}(\mathcal{D}_U)}{\gamma_{jm}^{\text{num}} + \alpha \gamma_{jm}^{\text{den}}(\mathcal{D}_U)} \quad (13)$$

$$\hat{\sigma}_{jm}^2 = \frac{\boldsymbol{s}_{jm}^{\text{num}} + \alpha \boldsymbol{s}_{jm}^{\text{den}}(\mathcal{D}_U)}{\gamma_{jm}^{\text{num}} + \alpha \gamma_{jm}^{\text{den}}(\mathcal{D}_U)} - \hat{\mu}_{jm}^2 \quad (14)$$

3 Results and Discussion

The purpose of designing the learning algorithms is for classification/recognition of speech sounds, so we conducted phonetic classification experiments using the TIMIT database (Garofolo et al., 1993). We would like to investigate the relation of learning capability of semi-supervised algorithms to other factors and generalize our observations to other data sets. Therefore, we used another synthetic dataset *Waveform* for the evaluation of semi-supervised learning algorithms for Gaussian Mixture model.

TIMIT: We used the same 48 phone classes and further grouped into 39 classes according to (Lee and Hon, 1989) as our final set of phone classes to model. We extracted 50 speakers out of the NIST complete test set to form the development set. All of our experimental analyses were on the development set. We used segmental features (Halberstadt, 1998) in the phonetic classification task. For each phone occurrence, a fixed-length vector was calculated from the frame-based spectral features (12 PLP coefficients plus energy) with a 5 ms frame rate and a 25 ms Hamming window. More specifically, we divided the frames for each phone into three regions with 3-4-3 proportion and calculated the PLP average over each region. Three averages plus the log duration of that phone gave a 40-dimensional $(13 \times 3 + 1)$ measurement vector.

Waveform: We used the second versions of the *Waveform* dataset available at the UCI repository (Asuncion and Newman, 2007). There are three classes of data. Each token is described by 40 real attributes, and the class distribution is even.

For *waveform*, because the class labels are equally distributed, we simply assigned equal number of mixtures for each class. For TIMIT, the phone classes are unevenly distributed, so we assigned variable number of Gaussian mixtures for each class by controlling the averaged data counts per mixture. For all experiments, the initial model is an MLE model trained with labeled data only.

To construct a mixed labeled/unlabeled data set, the original training set were randomly divided into the labeled and unlabeled sets with desired ratio, and the class labels in the unlabeled set are assumed to be unknown. To avoid that the classifier performance may vary with particular portions of data, we ran *five* folds for every experiment, each fold corresponding to different division of training data into labeled and unlabeled set, and took the averaged performance.

3.1 Model Complexity

This section analyzes the learning capability of semi-supervised learning algorithms for different model complexities, that is, the number of mixtures for Gaussian mixture model. In this experiment, the sizes of labeled and unlabeled set are fixed ($|D_L| : |D_U| = 1 : 10$ and the averaged token counts per class is around 140 for both data sets), as we varied the total number of mixtures and evaluated the updated model by its classification accuracy. For *waveform*, number of mixtures was set from 2 to 7; for TIMIT, because the number of mixtures per class is determined by the averaged data counts per mixture c, we set c to 25, 20 and 15 as the higher c gives less number of mixtures in total. Figure 3.1 plots the averaged classification accura-

Figure 1: Mean classification accuracies vs. α for different model complexity. The accuracies for the initial MLE models are indicated in the parentheses. (a) *waveform*: training with the hybrid objective. (b) *waveform*: purely generative objective. (c) TIMIT: training with the hybrid objective. (d) TIMIT: purely generative objective.

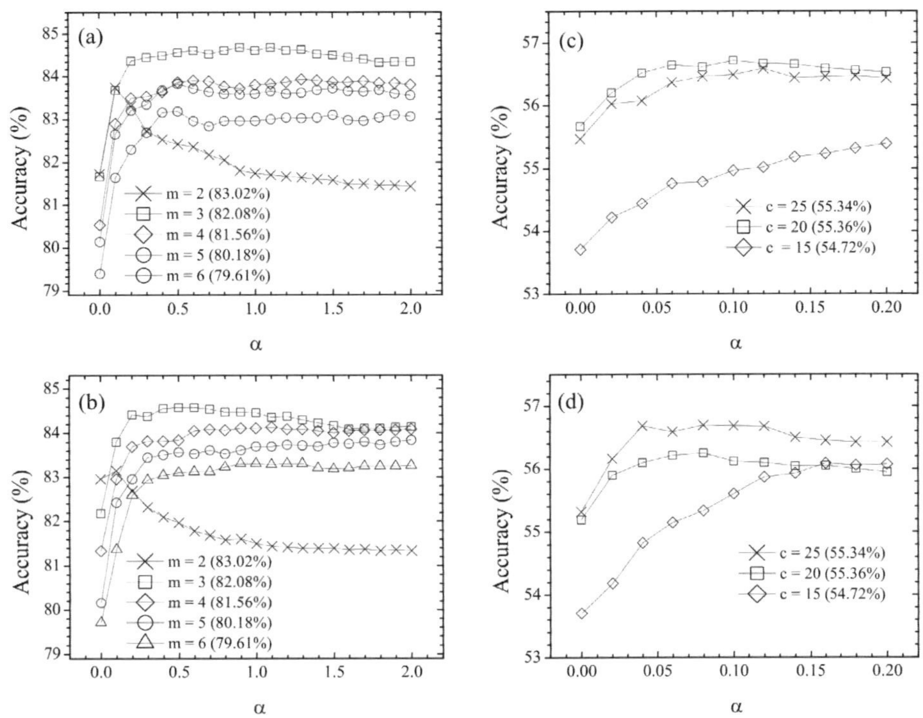

cies of the updated model versus the value of α with different model complexities. The ranges of α are different for *waveform* and TIMIT because the value of α for each dataset has different scales.

First of all, the hybrid method and purely generative method have very similar behaviors in both *waveform* and TIMIT; the differences between the two methods are insignificant regardless of α. The hybrid method with $\alpha = 0$ means supervised MMI-training with labeled data only, and the purely generative method with $\alpha = 0$ means extra several rounds of supervised MLE-training if the convergence criterion is not achieved. With the small amount of labeled data, most of hybrid curves start slightly lower than the purely generative ones at $\alpha = 0$, but increase to as high as the purely generative ones as α increases.

For *waveform*, the accuracies increase with α increases for all cases except for the 2-mixture model. Table 1 summarizes the numbers from Figure 3.1. Except for the 2-mixture case, the improvement over the supervised model ($\alpha = 0$) is positively correlated to the model complexity, as the largest improvements occur at the 5-mixture and 6-mixture model for the hybrid and purely generative method respectively. However, the highest complexity does not necessarily gives the best classification accuracy; the 3-mixture model achieves the best accuracy among all models after semi-supervised learning whereas the 2-mixture model is the best model for supervised learning using labeled data only.

Experiments on TIMIT show a similar behavior[1]; as shown in both Figure 3.1 and Table 2, the improvement over the supervised model ($\alpha = 0$) is also positively correlated to the model complexity,

[1]Note that our baseline performance (the initial MLE model) is much worse than benchmark because only 10% of the training data were used. We justified our baseline model by using the whole training data and a similar accuracy (74%) to other work (e.g. (Sha and Saul, 2007)) was obtained.

Table 1: The accuracies(%) of the initial MLE model, the supervised model ($\alpha = 0$), the best accuracies with unlabeled data and the absolute improvements (Δ) over $\alpha = 0$ for different model complexities for *waveform*. The bolded number is the highest value along the same column.

		Hybrid			Purely generative		
#. mix	init. acc.	$\alpha = 0$	best acc.	Δ	$\alpha = 0$	best acc.	Δ
2	**83.02**	**81.73**	83.74	2.01	**82.96**	83.14	0.18
3	82.08	81.66	**84.69**	3.03	82.18	**84.58**	2.40
4	81.56	80.53	83.93	3.40	81.34	84.13	2.79
5	80.18	80.14	83.82	3.68	80.16	83.84	**3.68**
6	79.61	79.40	83.19	**3.79**	79.71	83.31	3.60

Table 2: The accuracies(%) of the initial MLE model, the supervised model ($\alpha = 0$), the best accuracies with unlabeled data and the absolute improvements (Δ) over $\alpha = 0$ for different model complexities for TIMIT. The bolded number is the highest value along the same column.

		Hybrid			Purely generative		
c	init. acc.	$\alpha = 0$	best acc.	Δ	$\alpha = 0$	best acc.	Δ
25	55.34	55.47	56.58	1.11	**55.32**	**56.7**	1.38
20	**55.36**	**55.67**	**56.72**	1.05	55.2	56.25	1.05
15	54.72	53.71	55.39	**1.68**	53.7	56.09	**2.39**

as the most improvements occur at $c = 25$ for both hybrid and purely generative methods. The semi-supervised model consistently improves over the supervised model. To summarize, unlabeled data improve training on models of higher complexity, and sometimes it helps achieve the best performance with a more complex model.

3.2 Size of Unlabeled Data

In Figure 2, we fixed the size of the labeled set (4% of the training set) and plotted the averaged classification accuracies for learning with different sizes of unlabeled data. First of all, the hybrid method and purely generative method still behave similarly in both *waveform* and TIMIT. For both datasets, the figures clearly illustrate that more unlabeled data contributes more improvement over the supervised model regardless of the value of α. Generally, a data distribution can be expected more precisely with a larger sample size from the data pool, therefore we expect the more unlabeled data the more precise information about the population, which improves the learning capability.

3.3 Discussion of α

During training, the weighted sum of $\mathcal{F}_{\text{MMI}}$ and $\mathcal{F}_{\text{ML}}$ in equation (15) increases with iterations, however $\mathcal{F}_{\text{MMI}}$ and $\mathcal{F}_{\text{ML}}$ are not guaranteed to increase individually. Figure 3 illustrates how α affects the respective change of the two components for a particular setting for *waveform*. When $\alpha = 0$, the objective function does not take unlabeled data into account, so $\mathcal{F}_{\text{MMI}}$ increases while $\mathcal{F}_{\text{ML}}$ decreases. $\mathcal{F}_{\text{ML}}$ starts to increase for nonzero α; $\alpha = 0.01$ corresponds to the case where both objectives increases. As α keeps growing, $\mathcal{F}_{\text{MMI}}$ starts to decrease whereas $\mathcal{F}_{\text{ML}}$ keeps rising. In this particular example, $\alpha = 0.05$ is the critical value at which $\mathcal{F}_{\text{MMI}}$ changes from increasing to decreasing. According to our observation, the value of α depends on the dataset and the relative size of labeled/unlabeled data. Table 3 shows the critical values for *waveform* and TIMIT for different sizes of labeled data ($5, 10, 15, 20\%$ of the training set) with a fixed set of unlabeled data (80%.) The numbers are very different across the datasets, but there is a consistent pattern within the dataset–the critical value increases as the size of labeled set increases. One possible explanation is that α contains an normal-

Figure 2: Mean classification accuracies vs. α for different amounts of unlabeled data (the percentage in the training set). The averaged accuracy for the initial MLE model is 81.66% for *waveform* and 59.41% for TIMIT. (a) *waveform*: training with the hybrid objective. (b) *waveform*: purely generative objective. (c) TIMIT: training with the hybrid objective. (d) TIMIT: purely generative objective.

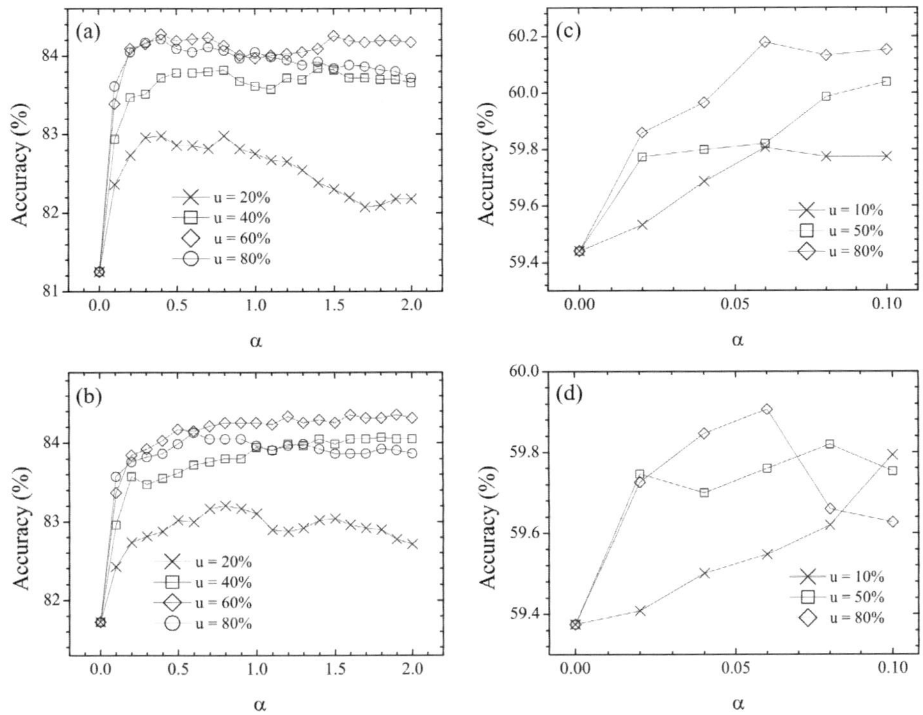

ization factor with respect to the relative size of labeled/unlabeled set. The objective function in (15) can be rewritten in terms of the normalized objective with respect to the data size:

$$\mathcal{F}(\lambda) = |D_L|\overline{\mathcal{F}}_{\text{MMI}}^{(D_L)}(\lambda) + \alpha|D_U|\overline{\mathcal{F}}_{\text{ML}}^{(D_U)}(\lambda). \quad (15)$$

where $\overline{\mathcal{F}}^{(X)}$ means the averaged value over the data set X. When the labeled set size increases, α may have to scale up accordingly such that the relative change of the two averaged component remains in the same scale.

Although α controls the dominance of the criterion on labeled data or on unlabeled data, the fact that which dominates the objective or the critical value does not necessary indicate the best α. However, we observed that the best α is usually close to or larger than the critical value, but the exact value varies with different data. At this point, it might still be easier to find the best weight using a small development set. But this observation also provides a guide about the reasonable range to search the best α – searching starting from the critical value and it should reach the optimal value soon according to the plots in Figure 3.1.

Table 3: The critical values for *waveform* and TIMIT for different sizes of labeled data (percentage of training data) with a fixed set of unlabeled data (80 %.)

Size of labeled data	*waveform*	TIMIT
5%	0.09-0.11	0.03-0.04
10%	0.12-0.14	0.07-0.08
15%	0.5-0.6	0.08-0.09
20%	1-1.5	0.11-0.12

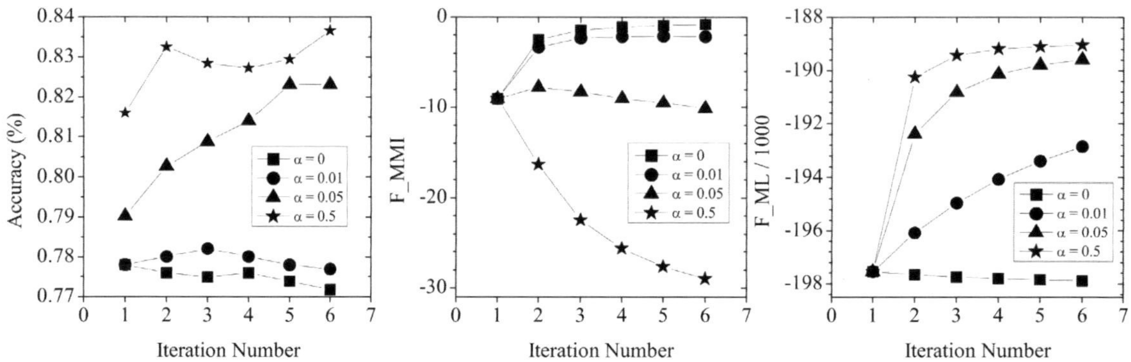

Figure 3: Accuracy (left), $\mathcal{F}_{\text{MMI}}$ (center), and $\mathcal{F}_{\text{ML}}$ (right) at different values of $alpha$.

3.4 Hybrid Criterion vs. Purely Generative Criterion

From the previous experiments, we found that the hybrid criterion and purely generative criterion almost match each other in performance and are able to learn models of the same complexity. This implies that the criterion on labeled data has less impact on the overall training direction than unlabeled data. In Section 3.2, we mentioned that the best α is usually larger than or close to the critical value around which the unlabeled data likelihood tends to dominate the training objective. This again suggests that labeled data contribute less to the training objective function compared to unlabeled data, and the criterion on labeled data doesn't matter as much as the criterion on unlabeled data. It is possible that most of the contributions from labeled data have already been used for training an initial MLE model, therefore little information could be extracted in the further training process.

4 Conclusion

Regardless of the dataset and the training objective type on labeled data, there are some general properties about the semi-supervised learning algorithms studied in this work. First, while limited amount of labeled data can at most train models of lower complexity well, the addition of unlabeled data makes the updated models of higher complexity much improved and sometimes perform better than less complex models. Second, the amount of unlabeled data in our semi-supervised framework generally follows 'the-more-the-better' principle; there is a trend that more unlabeled data results in more improvement in classification accuracy over the supervised model.

We also found that the objective type on labeled data has little impact on the updated model, in the sense that hybrid and purely generative objectives behave similarly in learning capability. The observation that the best α occurs after the MMI criterion begins to decrease supports the fact that the criterion on labeled data contributes less than the criterion on unlabeled data. This observation is also helpful in determining the search range for the best α on the development set by locating the critical value of the objective as a start point to perform search.

The unified training objective method has a nice convergence property which self-training methods can not guarantee. The next step is to extend the similar framework to speech recognition task where HMMs are trained and phone boundaries are segmented. It would be interesting to compare it with self-training methods in different aspects (e.g. performance, reliability, stability and computational efficiency).

References

A. Asuncion and D.J. Newman. 2007. UCI machine learning repository.

Gregory Druck, Chris Pal, Andrew McCallum, and Xiaojin Zhu. 2007. Semi-supervised classification with hybrid generative/discriminative methods. In *KDD '07: Proceedings of the 13th ACM SIGKDD international conference on Knowledge discovery and data mining*, pages 280–289, New York, NY, USA. ACM.

J. S. Garofolo, L. F. Lamel, W. M. Fisher, J. G. Fiscus, D. S. Pallett, and N. L. Dahlgren. 1993. Darpa timit acoustic phonetic continuous speech corpus.

Andrew K. Halberstadt. 1998. *Heterogeneous Acoustic Measurements and Multiple Classifiers for Speech Recognition*. Ph.D. thesis, Massachusetts Institute of Technology.

J.-T. Huang and Mark Hasegawa-Johnson. 2008. Maximum mutual information estimation with unlabeled data for phonetic classification. In *Interspeech*.

Masashi Inoue and Naonori Ueda. 2003. Exploitation of unlabeled sequences in hidden markov models. *IEEE Trans. On Pattern Analysis and Machine Intelligence*, 25:1570–1581.

Shihao Ji, Layne T. Watson, and Lawrence Carin. 2009. Semisupervised learning of hidden markov models via a homotopy method. *IEEE Trans. Pattern Anal. Mach. Intell.*, 31(2):275–287.

M.J.F. Gales L. Wang and P.C. Woodland. 2007. Unsupervised training for mandarin broadcast news and conversation transcription. In *Proc. IEEE Conference on Acoustics, Speech, and Signal Processing (ICASSP)*, volume 4, pages 353–356.

Lori Lamel, Jean-Luc Gauvain, and Gilles Adda. 2002. Lightly supervised and unsupervised acoustic model training. 16:115–129.

K.-F. Lee and H.-W. Hon. 1989. Speaker-independent phone recognition using hidden markov models. *IEEE Transactions on Speech and Audio Processing*, 37(11):1641–1648.

B. Merialdo. 1988. Phonetic recognition using hidden markov models and maximum mutualinformation training. In *Proc. IEEE Conference on Acoustics, Speech, and Signal Processing (ICASSP)*, volume 1, pages 111–114.

Daniel Povey. 2003. *Discriminative Training for Large Vocabulary Speech Recognition*. Ph.D. thesis, Cambridge University.

Fei Sha and Lawrence K. Saul. 2007. Large margin hidden markov models for automatic speech recognition. In B. Schölkopf, J. Platt, and T. Hoffman, editors, *Advances in Neural Information Processing Systems 19*, pages 1249–1256. MIT Press, Cambridge, MA.

Frank Wessel and Hermann Ney. 2005. Unsupervised training of acoustic models for large vocabulary continuous speech recognition. *IEEE Transactions on Speech and Audio Processing*, 13(1):23–31, January.

Discriminative Models for Semi-Supervised Natural Language Learning

Sajib Dasgupta and **Vincent Ng**
Human Language Technology Research Institute
University of Texas at Dallas
Richardson, TX 75083-0688
{sajib,vince}@hlt.utdallas.edu

1 Discriminative vs. Generative Models

An interesting question surrounding semi-supervised learning for NLP is: should we use discriminative models or generative models? Despite the fact that generative models have been frequently employed in a semi-supervised setting since the early days of the statistical revolution in NLP, we advocate the use of discriminative models. The ability of discriminative models to handle complex, high-dimensional feature spaces and their strong theoretical guarantees have made them a very appealing alternative to their generative counterparts. Perhaps more importantly, discriminative models have been shown to offer competitive performance on a variety of sequential and structured learning tasks in NLP that are traditionally tackled via generative models , such as letter-to-phoneme conversion (Jiampojamarn et al., 2008), semantic role labeling (Toutanova et al., 2005), syntactic parsing (Taskar et al., 2004), language modeling (Roark et al., 2004), and machine translation (Liang et al., 2006). While generative models allow the seamless integration of prior knowledge, discriminative models seem to outperform generative models in a "no prior", agnostic learning setting. See Ng and Jordan (2002) and Toutanova (2006) for insightful comparisons of generative and discriminative models.

2 Discriminative EM?

A number of semi-supervised learning systems can bootstrap from small amounts of labeled data using discriminative learners, including self-training, co-training (Blum and Mitchell, 1998), and transductive SVM (Joachims, 1999). However, none of them seems to outperform the others across different domains, and each has its pros and cons. Self-training can be used in combination with any discriminative learning model, but it does not take into account the confidence associated with the label of each data point, for instance, by placing more weight on the (perfectly labeled) seeds than on the (presumably noisily labeled) bootstrapped data during the learning process. Co-training is a natural choice if the data possesses two independent, redundant feature splits. However, this conditional independence assumption is a fairly strict assumption and can rarely be satisfied in practice; worse still, it is typically not easy to determine the extent to which a dataset satisfies this assumption. Transductive SVM tends to learn better max-margin hyperplanes with the use of unlabeled data, but its optimization procedure is non-trivial and its performance tends to deteriorate if a sufficiently large amount of unlabeled data is used.

Recently, Brefeld and Scheffer (2004) have proposed a new semi-supervised learning technique, EM-SVM, which is interesting in that it incorporates a discriminative model in an EM setting. Unlike self-training, EM-SVM takes into account the confidence of the new labels, ensuring that the instances that are labeled with less confidence by the SVM have less impact on the training process than the confidently-labeled instances. So far, EM-SVM has been tested on text classification problems, outperforming transductive SVM. It would be interesting to see whether EM-SVM can beat existing semi-supervised learners for other NLP tasks.

Proceedings of the NAACL HLT Workshop on Semi-supervised Learning for Natural Language Processing, pages 84–85,
Boulder, Colorado, June 2009.

3 Effectiveness of Bootstrapping

How effective are the aforementioned semi-supervised learning systems in bootstrapping from small amounts of labeled data? While there are quite a few success stories reporting considerable performance gains over an inductive baseline (e.g., parsing (McClosky et al., 2008), coreference resolution (Ng and Cardie, 2003), and machine translation (Ueffing et al., 2007)), there are negative results too (see Pierce and Cardie (2001), He and Gildea (2006), Duh and Kirchhoff (2006)). Bootstrapping performance can be sensitive to the setting of the parameters of these semi-supervised learners (e.g., when to stop, how many instances to be added to the labeled data in each iteration). To date, however, researchers have relied on various heuristics for parameter selection, but what we need is a principled method for addressing this problem. Recently, McClosky et al. (2008) have characterized the conditions under which self-training would be effective for semi-supervised syntactic parsing. We believe that the NLP community needs to perform more research of this kind, which focuses on identifying the algorithm(s) that achieve good performance under a given setting (e.g., few initial seeds, large amounts of unlabeled data, complex feature space, skewed class distributions).

4 Domain Adaptation

Domain adaptation has recently become a popular research topic in the NLP community. Labeled data for one domain might be used to train a initial classifier for another (possibly related) domain, and then bootstrapping can be employed to learn new knowledge from the new domain (Blitzer et al., 2007). It would be interesting to see if we can come up with a similar semi-supervised learning model for projecting resources from a resource-rich language to a resource-scarce language.

References

John Blitzer, Mark Dredze, and Fernando Pereira. 2007. Biographies, bollywood, boom-boxes and blenders: Domain adaptation for sentiment classification. In *Proceedings of the ACL.*

Avrim Blum and Tom Mitchell. 1998. Combining labeled and unlabeled data with co-training. In *Proceedings of COLT.*

Ulf Brefeld and Tobias Scheffer. 2004. Co-EM support vector learning. In *Proceedings of ICML.*

Kevin Duh and Katrin Kirchhoff. 2006. Lexicon acquisition for dialectal Arabic using transductive learning. In *Proceedings of EMNLP.*

Shan He and Daniel Gildea. 2006. Self-training and co-training for semantic role labeling.

Sittichai Jiampojamarn, Colin Cherry, and Grzegorz Kondrak. 2008. Joint processing and discriminative training for letter-to-phoneme conversion. In *Proceedings of ACL-08:HLT.*

Thorsten Joachims. 1999. Transductive inference for text classification using support vector machines. In *Proceedings of ICML.*

Percy Liang, Alexandre Bouchard, Dan Klein, and Ben Taskar. 2006. An end-to-end discriminative approach to machine translation. In *Proceedings of the ACL.*

David McClosky, Eugene Charniak, and Mark Johnson. 2008. When is self-training effective for parsing? In *Proceedings of COLING.*

Vincent Ng and Claire Cardie. 2003. Weakly supervised natural language learning without redundant views. In *Proceedings of HLT-NAACL.*

Andrew Ng and Michael Jordan. 2002. On discriminative vs.generative classifiers: A comparison of logistic regression and Naive Bayes. In *Advances in NIPS.*

David Pierce and Claire Cardie. 2001. Limitations of co-training for natural language learning from large datasets. In *Proceedings of EMNLP.*

Brian Roark, Murat Saraclar, Michael Collins, and Mark Johnson. 2004. Discriminative language modeling with conditional random fields and the perceptron algorithm. In *Proceedings of the ACL.*

Ben Taskar, Dan Klein, Michael Collins, Daphne Koller, and Christopher Manning. 2004. Max-margin parsing. In *Proceedings of EMNLP.*

Kristina Toutanova, Aria Haghighi, , and Christopher D. Manning. 2005. Joint learning improves semantic role labeling. In *Proceedings of the ACL.*

Kristina Toutanova. 2006. Competitive generative models with structure learning for NLP classification tasks. In *Proceedings of EMNLP.*

Nicola Ueffing, Gholamreza Haffari, and Anoop Sarkar. 2007. Transductive learning for statistical machine translation. In *Proceedings of the ACL.*

Author Index